Working with
Numbers and Statistics
A Handbook for Journalists

LEA'S COMMUNICATION SERIES

Jennings Bryant/Dolf Zillmann, General Editors

Selected titles in Journalism (Maxwell McCombs, Advisory Editor) include:

Friedmann/Dunwood/Rogers • Communicating Uncertainty: Media Coverage of News and Controversial Science

Garrison • Professional Feature Writing, Fourth Edition

Iorio • Taking It to the Streets: Qualitative Research in Journalism

Livingston/Voakes • Working with Numbers and Statistics

Merritt/McCombs • The Two W's of Journalism: The Why and What of Public Affairs Reporting

Roush • Show Me the Money: Writing Business and Economics Stories for Mass Communication

Salwen/Garrison/Driscoll • Online News and the Public

Titchener • Reviewing the Arts, Second Edition

For a complete list of titles in LEA's Communication Series, please contact Lawrence Erlbaum Associates, Publishers, at www.erlbaum.com.

Working with Numbers and Statistics

A Handbook for Journalists

Charles Livingston
Paul Voakes

 LAWRENCE ERLBAUM ASSOCIATES, PUBLISHERS
2005   Mahwah, New Jersey   London

Lawrence Erlbaum Associates, Inc., Publishers
10 Industrial Avenue
Mahwah, New Jersey 07430

Cover design by Melissa Cassutt
Page design by Elena A. Fraboschi

Library of Congress Cataloging-in-Publication Data

Livingston, Charles.
    Working with numbers and statistics: A handbook for journalists /
Charles Livingston, Paul Voakes.
        p. cm. – (LEA's communication series)
Includes bibliographical references and index.
ISBN 0-8058-5248-4 – ISBN 0-8058-5249-2 (alk. paper)
    1. Mathematics.   2. Statistics.   3. Journalism-Mathematics.
I. Voakes, Paul S. II. Title. III. Series.

QA39.2.L59 2004
510-dc22

                                                        2004054123

Contents

Preface

Our interest in writing a book about mathematics and statistics for journalists was inspired by our work designing and teaching a course for journalism students. The development of that course was supported by a Mathematics Throughout the Curriculum grant from the National Science Foundation, with Principal Investigator Dan Maki, professor of mathematics at Indiana University. We thank the NSF and Dan for their support.

Andrew Ellett, a mathematics graduate student at Indiana University, assisted us and later taught the math-stat journalism course. We learned a lot from Andrew about how to approach the educational needs of our audience, and he gave us excellent feedback on our efforts. Steve McKinley, a lecturer in the Department of Mathematics, also gave us valuable feedback, as did our colleague, Steen Andersson. We are grateful to Andrew, Steve and Steen for their contributions. Finally, one article, "How numbers can trick you" by Arnold Barnett (Technology Review, October 1994), was especially informative to us.

We have gained much from our students. Their feedback was invaluable as we learned to teach mathematics for journalists. This book is far better for our experiences with them.

The book was produced using the typesetting language LaTex. Elena Fraboschi designed the book and did the typesetting, transforming our bare-bones outline into what we hope the reader finds an attractive and appealing environment to enhance their understanding of mathematics and statistics.

Our deepest appreciation goes to our wives, Lynn Greenfield and Barbara Voakes, for their patience and encouragement during the development and writing of this book.

Working with Numbers and Statistics

A Handbook for Journalists

chapter

1

Introduction

Numbers, numbers, numbers. There's just no avoiding them, especially when you're a journalist. Numbers aren't just on the sports or financial pages. Whether you're reporting on local tax rates, medical research reports, school district budgets, environmental impact reports, box-office receipts, or any other subject most journalists consider newsworthy, the odds are good that you'll encounter numbers. And the odds are also good that you can tell the story better with the appropriate (and accurate) use of numbers.

This book had its origins in a course called Mathematics and Statistics for Journalism, at Indiana University. By 1999 the journalism faculty had begun to realize that their students, even when required to take math and statistics elsewhere on campus, were not applying any math skills to their reporting, writing, or editing classes. Meanwhile, Indiana's Department of Mathematics was coordinating a campuswide effort, funded by the National Science Foundation, to create math courses specific to other disciplines. Journalism was a natural for this project, and your two co-authors set about designing and teaching a course specifically for journalism majors.

We discovered in our students the same reluctance (some call it phobia) regarding math that we've seen among professional journalists over the years. After all, isn't this why many journalists became writers and editors in the first place, because science and math caused them to break out in hives?

❖ CHAPTER 1. INTRODUCTION ❖

Journalism students may not have realized it yet, but most professional journalists do recognize, perhaps grudgingly, how math skills make you a better journalist:

- You can make accurate, reliable computations, which in turn enable you to make relevant comparisons, put facts into perspective and lend important context to stories.
- You can protect yourself from being fooled by inaccurate presentations of data, whether willfully spun or just carelessly relayed. If we value independence as a cornerstone of journalism ethics, part of that independence must be the ability to assess numerical information without relying on the source.
- You can ask appropriate questions about numerical matters.
- You can translate complicated numbers for your viewers and readers, in ways they can readily understand. But it takes a full understanding on your part first.
- You can hold your own in the brave new world of computer-assisted reporting, which is no longer the preserve of newsroom geeks.
- Your writing can actually become livelier, because numbers give you precision, and precision always improves writing. Consider the following statements:

  "My husband is a moderate smoker."
  "I've read several books this summer."
  "The mayor has a comfortable income."

  So how many cigarettes a day does the husband smoke? How many books read? How much does the mayor make?

As simple and obvious as it may seem, numbers convey important meaning. But too often journalists skirt around the numerical parts of their fact-gathering and information-sharing, because they think they're incompetent with numbers.

This little book is designed to bolster a journalist's math skills, and in turn bolster a journalist's math confidence. We'll start with some math basics. It's been years, maybe decades, since you last computed a percentage change or found an average. For example, in seventh grade you were probably adept at figuring out the percentage change when a population has risen from 41,000 to 49,000. Every journalist should feel confident doing fairly simple procedures like that (and that's right; it was a 19.5 percent increase).

We'll also cover the basics of statistics, called descriptive statistics: the mathematical procedures people use to summarize vast amounts of data. For example, if Republicans claim the average salary of state workers is $37,000 and Democrats claim the average worker earns only $31,000, is one party lying? Not necessarily: One "average" could be the mean, and the other figure could be the median. Every journalist should know the difference between the two, and when sources might be tempted to use one or the other to their advantage.

Then we'll move slightly beyond the basics, to inferential statistics — the procedures people use to draw conclusions from the initial statistical findings. Even if they never compute statistics on their own, journalists need to know the basic language and logic of statistics. For example, if the latest poll has one candidate with 49 percent support of those likely to vote, and the other candidate with 47 percent, can we conclude that the first candidate holds a slim lead? No — at least not without a lot more information. Another example: If a national health survey finds that middle-aged men on the West Coast and Hawaii had less heart disease than middle-aged men in the Midwest and South, does that mean we should advise our viewers to go west (if they want to live longer)? No — there may be a more pertinent reason than geography for that difference.

We'll review some of the little things as well, like usage and style when you're writing with numbers. For example, which of the following is better writing?

The city council approved a budget increase
of $39.2 million.

The city council approved a budget increase
of 17 percent.

It's the second sentence, because the quantity 17 percent has more immediate meaning to readers than the quantity $39.2 million, especially with no more context than provided.

We've tried to provide the same basic structure in each of the chapters that follow. We'll always start with the math, so that if all you need is a reminder of something you learned long ago, you can plunge straight into it. If the key mathematical procedure is a fundamental formula or a rule of thumb, you'll find that displayed in a box. For every procedure we'll provide an example or two, to show how the math would be done in a specific situation. At the end of every section, we'll put the math into a more journalistic context, so you can see how the procedures are likely to come into play in the work of a reporter or editor.

We've tried to keep the statistics simple, telling you what you need to know to deal with the situations journalists are most likely to confront. But we've also added a chapter called Advanced Statistics, which elaborates on the basics from chapters 4 and 5.

This book is not designed as a math or stats textbook — there are plenty of those floating around college math departments — so you won't see practice problem sets or elongated examples. Rather we hope you'll keep this as a reference work for your bookshelf, right alongside your style book, dictionary, almanac and whatever other works you keep handy for daily use.

Without skills in math or stats, journalists constantly have to rely on the calculations and interpretations of their sources, and constantly hope and pray that the numbers they use in their writing are appropriate and correct. That situation presents a picture of neither independence nor accuracy. However, journalists armed with some logic, technique, and interpretive skills can analyze research, ask appropriate questions and understand the data well enough to tell readers and viewers clearly what the numbers mean. We hope this book can help you achieve those goals.

Summary of Chapters

Chapter 2 presents basic mathematical concepts; we haven't tried to give a review course in elementary mathematics, but rather have identified some of the topics that come up most frequently for journalists. Chapter 2 also presents some of the basic mathematics that arises in working with budgets, taxes, and in business reporting. Chapters 3, 4, 5, and 6as are the heart of our presentation on statistics: Chapter 3 tells you some of the tools used to describe data; Chapter 4 tells you how to use data to estimate unknown numbers; Chapter 5 describes how statistical methods permit you to draw inferences from those estimates and judge the reliability of those inferences; Chapter 6 describes surveying techniques, as surveys are the most important method used to gather data about large groups. Chapter 7 presents advanced topics in statistics, those that underlie the previous material and might arise occasionally for the journalist. In Chapter 8 each section is focused on a common misunderstanding that arises in the use of statistical methods, including an extended section on the contrast between "probability" and "odds." The concluding chapters are of independent interest: Chapter 9 summarizes the usefulness of computers to mathematical and statistical work of journalists: resources on the Internet and the use of Microsoft Excel in working with data; Chapter 10 focuses on the writing aspects of working with numbers.

In the text we use special icons to indicate examples and warnings:

☞ This icon denotes basic examples, often with mathematical content.

✎ This icon marks examples that are focused on writing issues.

↘ This icon indicates a warning.

chapter

2

Some Fundamentals

2.1. Percentages

Computing Percentages

> To convert a percentage to a (decimal) number, shift the decimal point two places to the left.

☞ 15 percent is the same as .15.

> To convert a decimal to the percentage, shift the decimal point two places to the right and add "percent."

☞ .49 is 49 percent.

> To compute a certain percentage of a certain number, multiply the number by the percentage in decimal form.

☞ To compute 75 percent of 200, multiply 200 by 75 percent, or .75, and you get 150. So 150 is 75 percent of 200.

> To compute a percentage when all you have is two numbers, divide the "portion" by the "whole."

☞ What percentage of 200 is represented by 30? Here 30 is the portion, and 200 is the whole. Dividing 30 by 200 yields .15, or 15 percent.

Sometimes the "whole" can actually be smaller than the "portion," but the same rule applies.

☞ What percentage of 200 is represented by 300? Here 200 is again the "whole" (because we want the percentage "of 200"), so divide 300 by 200 and you get 1.5. Shift the decimal point two places to the right and you get 150 percent.

Percentage Change

By how much did a budget, or a batting average, or a company's profit, go up or down? To calculate percentage changes, you need to focus on two key amounts: the amount of change, and the "old number" amount.

> To compute a percentage change, divide the amount of change by the "old number."

☞ The price of ZippyCar in 2002 was $18,000. In 2003 the price had increased to $19,200. What was the percentage increase? First, determine the amount of change and the "old number." In this example the "old number" is $18,000. To get the amount of change, subtract $18,000 from $19,200 and you get $1,200. Divide the amount of change by the "old number" ($1,200 divided by $18,000) and you get .067, or 6.7 percent. The price of the car had risen by nearly 7 percent.

☞ The price of a SnazzyCar in 2003 was 5 percent higher than its 2002 price of $14,000. What is the 2003 price? This time we have the "old number" ($14,000), but we also need the amount of change. You know the change is 5 percent, so just convert that to a raw number. To convert the 5 percent we simply multiply the "whole" ($14,000) by the percentage, which is the same as .05. That multiplication gives you $700, the amount of price change. So if the old price was $14,000 and the price went up by $700, then the new price is $14,700. **Negative Changes** If something decreases, its change is denoted with a negative number.

☞ If the price of gas one week was $1.49 and the next week it was $1.39, the change was −10 cents. This represented a percentage change of −.10/1.49 = −.067, or roughly a −6.7 percent change. This is usually referred to as a "6.7 percent decrease."

⤬ If a candidate's support has gone from 50 percent to 60 percent, you should say that it has gone up by "*10 percentage points*," not by 10 percent. Since 10 percent of 50 is 5, a 10 percent increase over 50 percent gives 55 percent, not 60!

See Chapter 8 for more about this issue.

Percentage Change: Backward

Sometimes you know the present value of something and what percentage change it represents over a previous amount, but not the previous amount. Here is an example illustrating how to work backwards to find that previous value.

☞ The 2003 price of a SizzlerCar was $22,575 and this represented a 5 percent increase over the 2002 price. What was the price of the 2002 SizzlerCar? Here a bit of algebra is unavoidable. We have that $22,575 = (2002 price) plus (.05)(2002 price). Do the algebra and you will find that (2002 price) = $22,575/1.05 = $21,500.

> If an amount B represents a p percent increase over a previous amount A, then $A = B/(1 + p)$. Remember: In performing the division, convert p to a decimal.

☞ The median salary of a clerical worker at TypingPoolCom this year is $28,345, an increase of 4 percent over last year. To find last year's median, compute $A = \frac{28,345}{1+.04} = \$27,255$.

✎ The percentage is one of the best (mathematical) friends a journalist can have, because it quickly puts numbers into context. And it's a context that the vast majority of readers and viewers can comprehend immediately. You could write,

"The number of expulsions from county high schools was up this year," or "County high schools expelled 52 more students this year than last year," or "County high schools expelled 132 students this year." But is that a lot of expulsions? A blessed few? Who knows?

There's more you can do to help readers and viewers make more sense of the numbers quickly: Express the change as a percentage. "County high schools expelled 132 students this year, a 65 percent increase over last year's expulsions." Suddenly readers and viewers appreciate that this was an important increase, without your having to sound like an editorialist (or alarmist) by using descriptors like "whopping." Let the percentage deliver the impact.

2.2. Adjusting for Inflation

In describing the change in price or other dollar amount over time, you may want to take into account the overall change in the cost of living — inflation. The Federal Bureau of Labor Statistics tracks the cost of living and keeps a historical record on its web site at http://stats.bls.gov/cpi. On page 109 we have listed the Consumer Price Index, the CPI, for each year from 1920 through 2004. Here's how to use it to adjust for inflation.

Understanding the CPI

In defining the CPI the bureau begins with a standard "market basket" of consumer goods. This includes basic foods, but also includes everything from transportation to housing expenses. Based on this market basket, an average price is computed. The procedure for computing the average is complicated; the goal is to achieve a number that, when computed from year to year, accurately reflects the overall change in costs faced by an average consumer in an urban community in the United States.

In its latest formulation, the Bureau of Labor statistics has adjusted the CPI to a scale for which the CPI was 100 in August 1983. This only has meaning when compared to the CPI for another year.

☞ According to the table in the Appendix on page 109, in January 1990 the CPI was 127.4; this means that, on average, prices had increased by 27.4 percent from August 1983 to January 1990.

Computing with the CPI

To work with the CPI it is useful to compute the *Inflation Factor* between the years of interest.

> Compute the Inflation Factor between two years by dividing the CPIs for the years.

☞ If we are comparing prices in 1976 to 2000 we divide the CPI for 2000, 168.7, by the CPI for 1976, 55.6. We find that the inflation factor from 1976 to 2000 is 3.03, or 303 percent; that is, prices in 2000 were roughly three times as high as in 1976.

☞ Suppose that you are writing an article about the change in the price of gasoline between 1976 and 2000. The January 1976 price of gasoline was 60 cents and the price of gasoline in January 2000 was $1.30. You can set both prices to 2000 prices by multiplying the 1976 price by the inflation factor, which was computed in the previous example to be 3.03. So, in "2000 dollars" the price of gasoline in 1976 was (3.03)(.60) = $1.82.

☞ Continuing with this example, if the price of gasoline in 2000 were $1.30, that would be 52 cents less than the price of gas in 1976, once that price was adjusted for inflation to be $1.82. The percentage change was .52/1.82 = .29, or 29 percent. That is, the price of gasoline in 2000 was 29 percent less than the price in 1976 after adjusting for inflation.

☞ Similarly, you can translate the 2000 price into 1976 dollars by dividing by the inflation factor. In the preceding example, the 2000 price of $1.30 yields a price of $1.30/3.03 = $.43 in 1976 dollars. Again, because 43 cents is less than 60 cents, we can conclude that gas is cheaper today, in "constant dollars."

✎ How many times have reporters heard politicians, board members or irate citizens grouse about the increase of a budget, or a public employee's salary, over the years? Does that mean you have to accept their outrage and pass it straight through to your readers or viewers? First you should do the math.

Let's say the average police officer's salary rose from $33,600 in 1981 to $61,400 in 2000. An outrageously large increase? Do the math and you'll see that these officers' salaries have not even kept pace with inflation. If they'd received cost-of-living increases each year equal to the rise in inflation, and no other kinds of raises, the average salary would be $65,200. You've still got a good story — but you might want to take a different angle.

2.3. Working with Probability

Probability is sometimes called the language of statistics. We all have an informal sense of the meaning of probability, for instance, when the weather report announces the chance of rain is 80 percent, we know to carry an umbrella. Here we want to highlight that the language is used in different ways, sometimes formal and sometimes not; the journalist needs to recognize which is which.

The *probability* of an event occurring might be described as the likelihood of it happening.

☞ If 3 out of every 10 new cars built by a certain company has a particular defect, then if a car from that company is selected at random, the probability of it having that defect is 3 out of 10, or $3/10 = .3$.

Probabilities may also be expressed as a percentage: in this case, the probability of finding a defect is 30 percent.

In a formal sense the word "probability" is used only when an event or experiment is repeatable and the long term likelihood of a certain outcome can be determined. For instance, we could repeatedly sample cars from a number of dealers in different locations, and if the probability of .3 is correct, we would find that roughly three tenths of the cars would have the defect.

The word "probability" is sometimes used in an informal sense.

> The probability that humans will walk on the
> moon again before 2020 is 90 percent.

This does not describe a repeatable event; either the event will occur or it will not. In this sense the writer is only indicating that another visit to the moon is likely.

In reporting, do not use the informal notion of probability.

In the previous situation it would be best to state it as follows:

> Given the goals of NASA and the level of gov-
> ernmental support, a visit to the moon seems
> likely in the next 15 years.

In the case of the weather report's "80 percent chance of rain tomorrow," the situation is repeatable in the sense that such predictions are made frequently, actually daily in thousands of different locations, and meteorological techniques are such that of all the predictions of "80 percent chance of rain," roughly 80 percent of the time the predictions are correct.

✎ Many a reporter has embarrassed his or her newsroom by confusing probability with quantity. You've probably seen the enterprise story about "the most dangerous stretch of road in the county." The story declares, for example, that "your chances of being involved in a fatal accident on Winding Way are greater than on any other stretch of road in the county." The data? The reporter has discovered that the number of fatal wrecks on Winding Way (seven deaths) was higher than the number for any other road in the county last year. But wait. Top quantity, yes, but highest likelihood? To predict likelihood, you'd have to know how many cars traveled Winding Way during that year. It's entirely possible that Winding Way had a high number of car-trips that year as well (say 70,000 car-trips). That would put the fatality rate at .0001, or one hundreth of 1 percent. If Dry Gulch Road had only two fatalities last year but only 5,000 car-trips, its fatal-crash rate was .0004, or four hundreths of 1 percent. In proportion to the amount of traffic, fatal wrecks on Dry Gulch were four times more common than wrecks on Winding Way, so should Winding Way be getting the "most dangerous" label?

2.4. Interest, Simple and Compound

From Wall Street to Main Street to anyone's stack of monthly bills, interest is of interest. The interest rate is the arbiter of the world of finance, at any level.

Interest is a fee a borrower pays a lender in return for the immediate use of the money. The amount of money borrowed is the principal, and the rate is the percentage of principal charged for the use of the money. Interest is expressed as an annual rate.

☞ If a consumer borrows $10,000 at an annual interest rate of 12 percent, she will owe $1,200 in interest at the end of one year in addition to the $10,000 principal she still owes. This is what's known as "simple" interest.

Computing interest is usually not so simple, because interest is usually "compounded." That means that the stated rate is divided up into smaller portions and added to the principal at stipulated times.

☞ In the previous example, if the 12 percent interest is compounded monthly, 1 percent is added to the principal each month. After one month the debt has gone up to $10,100, the original $10,000 plus the 1 percent interest charge. After another month it grows to $10,201. That's the $10,100 plus 1 percent of $10,100, which is $101. If you repeat this calculation 10 more times, you will find that the debt after a year is $11,268.

In this example, because of compounding, the interest charged is the same as if there was a simple annual interest rate of 12.68 percent. On bank accounts the distinction between the stated interest rate and the the effect of compounding is described with the "APY," the "annual percentage yield." In this language a bank might announce that its CD that pays 12 percent compounded monthly has an APY of 12.68 percent.

The effect of compounding can be dramatic, but it tapers off as the interval of compounding becomes very small. For instance, a 5 percent interest rate on a certificate of deposit, compounded monthly, has an APY of 5.12 percent. Compounded daily it has an APY of 5.13.

Similarly, a credit card having an annual interest rate of 18 percent compounded monthly has an effective rate of 19.56 percent. Compounded daily the effective rate becomes 19.72 percent.

2.5. Rates (Ratios)

Rates (or ratios) are handy ways of expressing mathematical relationships with a single, simple, standardized number. When the quantities start getting huge, such as reporting there are 32,156 straight-A students in the state's high-school population of 1.2 million students, it's easier on readers and listeners to report that one out of every 37 high school students in the state made straight A's this year.

The other reason rates and ratios are useful is that they enable comparisons to be made among figures from different times or places. Was Tombstone, Arizona, a more dangerous place to live or visit in the 1880s than New Orleans in the 1990s? How is it possible to answer that question when those periods are 110 years and 1,500 miles apart? Let's say historical records showed an average of 400 murders a year in New Orleans in the 1990s, and an average of 15 murders a year in Tombstone in the 1880s. In New Orleans you'd be far more likely to be murdered, right? Here's where the ratio comes in: it puts both figures on the same scale, in this case the scale of "murders per resident."

The math for finding a "per person" ratio is simple:

Per Person Ratio = Number of occurrences divided by population.

Given New Orleans' population of 500,000, we'd get a ratio of .0008, or "eight-hundredths of 1 percent of a murder" for every resident of the city. Because that's a ridiculously small number to most readers or listeners, let's multiply that result by 10,000, and we get eight murders for every 10,000 residents of New Orleans. That still seems more dangerous than Tombstone, with its mere 15 murders for the entire population. But now calculate the per-person ratio for Tombstone, with its population of 2,250 in 1880. The division yields .0067, and if we multiply that by 10,000 we get 67 murders for every 10,000 people — stupendously more frequent than the rate in New Orleans in the 1990s.

2.6. Scientific Notation

Archimedes invented it 2,500 years ago, and it still is used today. You won't have to write using scientific notation, but you might be called on to read it and translate it for your viewers or readers. Here's how it works.

- 10^n means 1 followed by n zeros.

$$10^2 = 100$$
$$10^8 = 100,000,000$$
$$10^0 = 1$$

- If the n is negative, it tells you how many places to the right of the decimal place the 1 falls.

$$10^{-1} = .1$$
$$10^{-3} = .001$$

- Usually scientific notation is combined with multiplication.

$$1.34 \cdot 10^4 = 1.34 \cdot 10,000 = 13,400$$
$$.45 \cdot 10^3 = .45 \cdot 1,000 = 450$$

- **Shortcut** Given $a \cdot 10^n$, write this out by writing down a and moving its decimal n places to the right or left, depending on whether n is positive or negative, respectively. In either case, zeros might have to be appended, as in the second two examples below.

$$1.425 \cdot 10^2 = 142.5$$
$$1.425 \cdot 10^4 = 14,250$$
$$2.34 \cdot 10^{-3} = .00234$$

2.7. Names of Numbers

In the USA:

thousand =	$1,000$	$= 10^3$
million =	$1,000,000$	$= 10^6$
billion =	$1,000,000,000$	$= 10^9$
trillion =	$1,000,000,000,000$	$= 10^{12}$

In Great Britain:

$$\begin{aligned}
\text{thousand} &= & 1,000 &= 10^3 \\
\text{million} &= & 1,000,000 &= 10^6 \\
\text{thousand million} &= & 1,000,000,000 &= 10^9 \\
\text{billion} &= & 1,000,000,000,000 &= 10^{12}
\end{aligned}$$

✎ Scientific notation usually signals extremely large or extremely small quantities, so take care that your translation, even if accurate, makes sense to readers or viewers. For example, if you're covering a research report that uses 10^{18}, you're not helping readers by translating that to such a large figure as 1,000,000,000,000,000,000. Nor are you helping much by writing "one quintillion." Use more familiar math terms to express the magnitude of the amount, such as "a million trillions." (A million trillion is the product of 10^6 and 10^{12}, and to multiply in scientific notation, you add the exponents: $(10^6)(10^{12}) = 10^{6+12} = 10^{18}$.)

Writing with Analogies

The magnitude of numbers, such as a billion or a trillion, may not be familiar to your readers. Using analogies helps.

☞ There are 60 seconds in a minute, 60 minutes in an hour, 24 hours in a day, 365 days in a year, and roughly 225 years since the U.S. independence. Multiply it all together to find that there are roughly $7 \cdot 10^9$ seconds since the U.S. independence. The U.S. budget deficit is roughly $7 trillion, or $7 \cdot 10^{12}$ dollars. So by dividing we get a quotient of 10^3, or one thousand. (To divide in scientific notation, subtract the exponents: $10^{12}/10^9 = 10^{12-9} = 10^3$.) So there is the analogy: "If Paul Revere had wanted to save enough money to pay off the $7 trillion U.S. deficit today, he would have needed to put aside $1,000 every second for the last 225 years."

2.8. Rounding

Most of your readers don't want to know that the city budget is $14,350,673 this year. You need to round. How many digits you keep depends on a number of factors, but how you throw away the rest is given by a formal rule.

> – If the part you are rounding away begins with a 4 or less, just remove it.
> – If the part you are rounding away begins with a 5 or more, increase the final digit of your rounded number by 1.

☞ $14,350,673 rounds to $14 million. The 350,673 is just thrown away because it begins with a 3.

☞ $14,350,673 rounds to $14.4 million (instead of 14.3) because the piece being thrown away, 50,673, begins with a 5.

↖ Sometimes rounding will lead to small apparent errors in sums. In this case, explain the source of the error.

☞ Of 11 schools, 5 are elementary (45 percent after rounding), 3 are junior high (27 percent after rounding) and 3 are high schools (again 27 percent). But 45 + 27 + 27 = 99, not 100 as expected. Explain: "Percentages don't add to 100 because of rounding."

✎ So how crudely do you round when you round off numbers? There are no hard and fast rules, as a lot depends on the audience for the story. For a general-circulation readership, these levels of details will usually suffice:

For decimals: Give no more than one decimal place, unless the second place is important to the story. Not "$32.397 million," just "$32.4 million." But "the council increased the police budget only from $1.71 million to $1.74 million."

For large numbers: Not "in front of 54,297 fans" but "in front of 54,000 fans" (unless for some reason those lopped-off 297 are key to understanding the writer's point).

Not "the city, with 647,901 residents," but "the city, with nearly 648,000 residents. . . "

Not "a budget of $1,851,978" but "a budget of $1.9 million" (or, if the details matter, as in the police-budget example above, then "$1.85 million").

This rounding is done primarily to help your audience process the information you're reporting — not for the sake of excusing reporters from using calculators. When you must calculate detailed amounts for a result you'll be putting in your story, don't round off those amounts at all. The more you round off during calculation, the greater the chance of a gross "rounding error" in your final result.

2.9. Conversion Factors

The Internet now offers web pages, easily found with a search engine, to assist you in converting from one unit of measurement to another. Here we present some of the most common conversion factors. The following lists gives the factors which you use to convert from one common unit of measurement to another. These are *multiplication* factors. To convert in the other direction, divide by the given factor.

☞ For instance, 5 miles converts to 8 kilometers, since 5(1.61) is approximately 8. In the other direction, to convert 10 kilometers to miles, divide 10 by 1.61 to get 6.2.

Distance.

Miles to Kilometers: 1.61
Yards to Meters: .914
Inches to Centimeters: 2.54
Miles to Feet: 5,280
Kilometers to Meters: 1000
Meters to Centimeters: 100
Yards to Feet: 3
Meters to Microns: 10^6

Mass.

Pounds to Kilograms: .454
Pounds to Ounces: 16
Tons to Pounds: 2000
British Tons to Pounds: 2240
Kilograms to Grams: 1000
Grams to Milligrams: 1000

Volume.

Gallons to Liters 3.79
Gallons to Quarts: 4
Quarts to Cups: 4
Pints to Cups: 2
Cups to Ounces: 16
Ounces to Tablespoons: 2
Tablespoons to Teaspoons: 3

Cubic Yards to Gallons: 202
Barrels to Gallons: 42

Velocity.
Miles per Hour to Kilometers per Hour: 1.61
Miles per Hour to Feet per Second: 1.47

Area.
Square Miles to Acres: 640
(An acre is roughly the area of a square with sides 70 yards.
    It is also roughly the area of a football field.)
Square Kilometers to Hectares: 100
Hectares to Acres: 2.47

Temperature.
To convert the temperature given in Celsius to Fahrenheit,
    multiply the temperature by 9/5 and add 32. (So, 20
    degrees C. is the same as $\frac{9}{5}(20) + 32 = 68$ degrees F.)
To convert the temperature given in Fahrenheit to Celsius,
    subtract 32 and multiply by 5/9. (So, 95 degrees F. is
    the same as $\frac{5}{9}(95 - 32) = 35$ degrees C.)

Handy *conversion calculators* (that sometimes include some ar-
cane units of measurement) are available on the Web. One
good one can be found at http://www.onlineconversion.com;
other conversion calculators can be found in a search of the
Web.

Combining Conversions

To convert from one measure to another you have to make
several calculations.

☞ How many centimeters are there in 1 foot? Using our
charts, first convert 1 foot to .333 yards (divide by 3). Then
convert .333 yards to .305 meters (multiply by .914). Finally,
convert .305 meters to 30.5 centimeters (multiply by 100).

☞ How many feet are there in 1,600 meters? First convert
to yards: 1,600 meters = 1,750.55 yards. (Divide by .914.)
Then multiply by 3 to convert yards to feet, and get 5,250 feet.
Notice that because a mile is 5,280 feet, a mile is roughly 30
feet longer than 1,600 meters.

Caution with Area

In general, if the linear dimensions of a region are doubled, the area goes up by a factor of 4. More generally, if the linear dimensions are mulitplied by a factor of r, the area is multiplied by a factor of r^2.

☞ A shopper is deciding between a 20-inch diagonal television and a 24-inch diagonal. The linear dimension has increased by a factor of $\frac{24}{20} = \frac{6}{5} = 1.2$, that is, an increase of 20 percent. Hence, the area of the large set is $(\frac{6}{5})^2 = 1.44$ times that of the smaller set, an increase of 44 percent.

☞ An acre is the area of a square plot of land with each side about 70 yards. Hence, a square plot with sides 140 yards will be about 4 acres. To find the side of a square with area 2 acres (double the area of the acre square), one has to multiply by a number, r, with square 2; that is, $r = \sqrt{2} = 1.4$ roughly. Hence the square with area two acres has sides of about $(70)(1.4) = 98$ yards.

✎ When to convert units of measurement? Again, a lot depends on your audience. If you sense your readers or listeners are more comfortable with milliliters than with fluid ounces, use millimeters. But American audiences, by and large, have not gone metric. Providing the conversion is often helpful. Most style books recommend using the unit of measurement your source has used, and then converting that for your audience if need be. For example, "In a speech yesterday, the agricultural minister said the land reform program provides sharecroppers each with up to two hectares — roughly five acres — of their own farm land."

Most style books also advise, however, that you not use your sources' abbreviations for metric units, such as kg, km or t (metric ton), in news copy. The common exception is mm (millimeter) in reference to film width or weapons.

2.10. Issues of Logic

There is one issue of logic that can lead to confusion, that of *implication*.

Reverse Implication

> To say that "*A* implies *B*" (or "if *A* then *B*")
> means simply that anytime *A* occurs, *B* also
> occurs.

To say "if it is raining then I carry an umbrella" simply means that whenever it rains, I have my umbrella. To say that "if George is the quarterback, the team wins" means simply that whenever George is the quarterback, his team wins.

The common error is to assume that it also means that whenever *B* occurs *A* also occurs. But just because I am carrying an umbrella, you cannot conclude that it is raining; I might carry my umbrella every day, whether it is raining or not, just to be careful. And, just because the team won, you cannot conclude that George was the quarterback; the team might have two or three excellent quarterbacks.

Though in these simple settings the flaw in reasoning is obvious, the mistake appears in print frequently.

Implication and Causation

> Saying that "*A* implies *B*" is not the same as
> saying that "*A* causes *B*."

Suppose that I only wear my hat on sunny days. That is, if you see me wearing my hat, you know that it is sunny; anytime I am wearing my hat you conclude that it is a sunny day. That is, my wearing a hat implies that it is sunny. Obviously my wearing a hat does not cause the day to be sunny.

✎ This problem occurs more often than it should in sports and political reporting. An analyst discovers that in any year in which the Bulldogs football team played on a Monday night in September, they have ended up with a losing record for the season. The temptation is to predict that "the Bulldogs are likely to do poorly this year because there's a Monday night game scheduled in September." The historical connection is certainly an oddity, but can this one quirk of scheduling really be expected to cause a losing season?

In politics, an analyst discovers that "in the last seven gubernatorial elections the candidate who carries small, rural Polk County wins the statewide election." By what logic is Polk County's result influencing the voting in the rest of the state? Not much logic at all.

2.11. Decoding Budgets

A budget — whether a school district's budget, a corporation's budget, a sports franchise's budget or a church's budget — is an organization's most concise statement of its values and priorities. It's also a detailed statement of the organization's plan for the current (or coming) year. Later we explain where the organization hopes to get its money, and how it intends to spend its money. But it's not always the simplest document to decipher, as each organization uses its own jargon and shorthand to describe its earning and spending categories. The key to understanding and reporting budgets, however, is context. The numbers will mean little to readers or viewers without a comparison to other budgets, so the first order of business is often to obtain the organization's budgets from the previous year (or years), to determine whether certain departments or activities will be spending more, or spending less, or will be eliminated (or whether new spending activities are being created). Here are a few budget basics:

Expenditures

This is a numerical summary of where the money will be spent. In both government budgets and business budgets, two important types of spending are summarized in the operating budget and in the capital budget. The operating budget refers to the costs of providing services, manufacturing products, paying salaries and benefits and all the other ongoing, year-to-year activities of the organization. The capital budget refers to the expenses involved with major physical changes for the organization: a new sanctuary for the church, a new bridge for the county, renovating a factory for the business. Again, look first for any significant increases or decreases in spending categories, compared to previous years.

Revenues

This is a numerical summary of how the organization plans to acquire the income it will need to implement the expenditures plan. For businesses, the principal source of income is usually sales. For government agencies, income usually is derived from taxes. City and county governments and school districts usually derive income from property taxes and user fees, while state and federal governments get their revenues from income tax. Some institutions have special revenue streams, such as tuition for colleges and universities.

✎ Because context is so important in understanding and reporting budgets, here are a few tips for transforming a look at a budget into an interesting article:

- Look not only for changes from the previous year, but also changes over several years. For example, you may see that the Parks & Recreation Department's spending for swimming-pool maintenance is $85,000 this year, down from $87,000 last year. That's only about a 2 percent decrease — hardly a story. But if you look at the budget from five years ago and see that the same "budget line" was $103,000, and 10 years ago it was $123,000, you can see that the swimming pool maintenance budget has evaporated by 31 percent over the last 10 years. With this perspective, now you may have an interesting story. By obtaining four or more budgets, it becomes easy to spot trends in an organization's spending habits, or in its sources of income.
- Another useful comparison is dollars spent vs. people served. For example, if the soup kitchen's budget shows $187,000 to be spent on the food used to prepare meals for the city's hungry and homeless, you may want to see other documents tallying the numbers of people and meals served. If those $187,000 provided 125 different people with 4,190 meals in a year, the soup kitchen is spending nearly $1,500 per client and $45 per meal served. That may be a story — but a story you couldn't get without the additional data. Now let's say the soup kitchen used that food budget to provide 93,900 meals to 1,000 people. The

average cost of food per meal is now about $2 and the cost per client is under $100. Again, you've got yourself a story.

- There may be several organizations in your area with similar characteristics. For example, a suburban city is budgeting $3.2 million for police services this year. You notice that there are five other suburban cities in the region with roughly the same population. Their police budgets, you discover, range from $700,000 to $2.1 million. Why is the first city's police budget so high? You may have a story.
- It is often useful to compare a budget's growth rate to other growth rates. For example, you may discover that the city's budget for police services has grown by 41 percent over the last 10 years. Look at the city's overall population growth. What if it has grown by only 5 percent in the same period? In pursuing an explanation for that discrepancy in growth rates, you're pursuing a good story. In situations such as this, don't forget to adjust for inflation too.

2.12. Taxes

As in so many other aspects of our existence, death and taxes are unavoidable in journalism. Most journalists, however, are much more comfortable writing an obituary than a story requiring tax figures. The good news is that taxes can be computed and explained with a basic knowledge of percentages and rates.

Sales Tax

The most straightforward means of taxation is sales tax. If a county's sales tax is 6 percent, for example, a consumer will pay 6 cents for every dollar of goods or services purchased (assuming the goods or purchases are not exempt from the sales tax).

✎ Let's say the county wants to raise its revenues by raising the sales tax from 6 percent to 7 percent. A good approach is to put the change into the context of a familiar purchase: "If the county approves the change, the sales tax on a $25,000 automobile will rise from $1,500 to $1,750."

Income taxes

Income tax is also a matter of percentages, but unlike the sales tax, income tax rates vary according to the characteristics of each taxpayer. In general, lower-income taxpayers pay a lower percentage of income when they pay their taxes, and higher-income taxpayers pay a higher percentage. And different taxpayers qualify for different deductions and tax credits. So take care in making judgments across the board whenever income-tax policy is the subject. Also, care is required in using tax rates to compute total taxes — it is essential to understand how *tax brackets* work. An example will illustrate the complexity.

Federal tax rates on *taxable income* for 2003 are presented in the abbreviated Table 1. So, based on this table how much does a married couple with a taxable income of $80,000 owe in taxes? At first glance it might seem to be $20,000, 25 percent of $80,000. But that is not correct.

Single Filers	Married Filing Jointly	Tax Rate
Up to $7,000	Up to $14,000	10%
$7,001 - $28,400	$14,001 - $56,800	15%
$28,401 - $68,800	$56,801 - $114,650	25%

TABLE 1. Tax Rate Table

To compute the taxes owed by this couple, you must break their income up into pieces, according to the brackets. That is, the first $14,000 of their taxable income is taxed at the 10 percent rate. The next $42,800 (the portion between $14,000 and $56,800) is taxed at the 15 percent rate. The final $23,200 (the portion between the $56,800 cut-off and their total) is taxed at the 25 percent rate. Thus, in combining these you find that their total tax is given by:

$$.1(\$14,000) + .15(\$42,800) + .25(\$23,200) = \$13,620.$$

This amount represents only 17 percent of their taxable income, but it is important to notice that for each additional $100 the couple earns, their taxes will go up by $25.

Notice too that this calculation hides the complexity of the tax system, since it is based on the *taxable income* rather than the *gross income*, and thus does not reveal the range of adjustments and deductions.

Property taxes

Property tax is often the principal source of income for city and county governments, and for school districts and other local jurisdictions. Despite its sometimes-imposing jargon, the math is fairly simple. Most property tax is based on the property's assessed value. A common rookie mistake is to equate the assessed with the market value, which is often much higher. The assessed value is set by the staff of a county's assessor, and it is based on a number of specific characteristics of a house or a business. Thus a person may have bought her condominium for $150,000, but the condo's assessed value (a matter of public record in the county offices, by the way) may be only $125,000. So if the property tax rate in that city were 1 percent, the condo owner would not be paying $1,500 in property taxes (based on what she paid for the condo) but rather $1,250 (based on the officially assessed value of the condo). In many American cities and counties, the unit of taxation on property is the mill. This is a unit equal to $1 for every $1,000 of assessed valuation. If, for example, a school district raises its property tax rate from five mills to seven mills, local property owners will now be paying $7 for every $1,000 of assessed value of their property.

> To compute property tax, multiply the millage rate by the assessed value of the property and divide by 1,000.

Many local jurisdictions have done away with the language of millage and simply state a rate "per $1,000 of assessed valuation." Regardless of the language, the computation is the same: It's always based on a set ratio.

✎ It's always a good approach to translate millage as soon as possible in the reporting of property tax news. Instead of writing, "The school district is raising property taxes from five to seven mills next year, which means property owners will be paying two dollars more for every $1,000 of assessed valuation," try something more familiar to readers:

"The school district is raising property taxes from five to seven mills next year, which means the owners of a home assessed at $250,000 will see their annual school taxes rise from $1,250 to $1,750."

2.13. Business Basics

The reporting of business news offers its own special challenges. We can't possibly cover all the math you'll ever encounter on the business or finance beat, but here are some basic explanations of fairly common situations, which can at least prepare you for higher levels later on — and save you some grief and embarrassment in the meantime.

Annual Reports/Financial Statements

The financial statement is an incredibly concise statement of how a company has been doing lately. A good place to start is in the company's most recent annual report (although sometimes it makes more sense to look at the latest quarterly report, depending on the story you're working on).

More and more of these are available on the companies' websites, immediately and free of charge. Once you've reached the website, usually you'll click on "Investor Relations." Or, go to www.reportgallery.com for links to more than 2,000 U.S. corporations. For the latest stock price information on a company there are many sources, but www.Hoovers.com has a good combination of company capsule summaries, recent news and today's stock prices, free of charge. An even easier-to-use site for beginners is http://moneycentral.msn.com/investor/.

The gravest math mistake for beginning business reporters is to misread the financial statement's unit of measurement. Often the numbers in the table are stated "in thousands of dollars," as a note in fine print near the bottom of the page will explain. This means that the figure in the statements for net sales, for example, may be $4,600,000, or what appears to be $4.6 million. But remember that these figures are "in thousands of dollars," which means you should add three zeroes to just about everything you see on the page. So the company had not $4.6 million in sales; it had $4.6 billion.

The first figure reporters usually scrutinize is *net income*, which means profit. Here's how the accountants figured it: They took the income from sales of the products or services, and then subtracted the cost and expenses, which include the cost of making the products they sold (cost of sales), the costs of marketing and administration, and other miscellaneous business costs. That's usually not the whole picture, though. Most companies have other costs, such as repayment of long-term loans and payment of income taxes, which must also be subtracted from the revenues. These computations result in "net income," also known as "net earnings."

Sometimes (unlike in most journalistic reporting) parentheses are more important than normal text. The parentheses mean that figure is a negative amount. If we were to see a company's net income listed as ($207,000), we'd be looking at an actual loss of $207 million, assuming that the net income is given in thousands of dollars. If companies report their net incomes in parentheses for too many quarters in a row, they'll soon be filing for bankruptcy.

Business analysts love the ratio. "Net income per share" often appears in a financial statement. If it shows $1.50, for example, it is reporting that for every share of the company's stock being traded on the stock market, the company earned a profit of about $1.50. As with all reporting of budgets and business, be mindful of changes over time. The earnings-per-share ratio means little in isolation, but if that ratio has been increasing in each of the last four years, then the company is indeed improving. But beware again: The "net income per share" is usually the only figure on the page that is not "in thousands of dollars," but simply in the amounted actually stated.

News from The Stock Market

Obviously, the travails of the stock market affect business reporting regularly. Here are a few basics.

The price of the stock fluctuates throughout each day according to the basic laws of supply and demand. What increases the demand for a particular stock is anyone's guess, but when demand goes up the price goes up. When the same upward or downward trend occurs in the prices of a large number of stocks representing several sectors of business and industry, then the stock market's performance becomes a big story.

Most stock-market news refers to the Dow Jones Industrial Average, and whether it's up or down. It's a measure of the performance of 30 selected industrial companies' stock, run through a complex formula, yielding a figure that is meaningless except in the context of past Dow Jones averages. And in that context it can be very meaningful. Those 30 stocks represent about one-fifth of the value of all U.S. stocks, and about a quarter of the value of the stocks on the New York Stock Exchange.

But it's not the only game in town. Dow Jones also figures daily averages for transportation, utilities, and indexes for about a dozen more categories of companies. Also commonly used are the Nasdaq index, Standard & Poor's index of 500 companies, the NYSE composite index, the Value Line index, the AMEX composite, and so on. So if you want to track the fate of, say, the computer industry's stocks, you can do better than just tracking the Dow Jones, the lumbering giants of American industry. You could track Nasdaq's computer index. For example, if a computer company in your area is down (in its stock price) by 25 percent since Jan. 1, your first reaction is to think of this company's stock as a disaster, especially when you see that Dow Jones is down only 17 percent since Jan. 1. But look at Nasdaq's computer index. It could be down by 40 percent since Jan. 1, so in relation to most computer companies, your local firm isn't doing badly.

✎ Here's a great example of when percentage change works better than actual raw numbers. Forty years ago, the news that the Dow gained 60 points in one day was spectacular. That's no longer the case, because the average has risen so steeply in the past 20 years. If the Dow "shot up" 60 points today, it might be more helpful to people to report that the Dow edged up two-thirds of 1 percent, which is what 60 points amounted to in late 2002.

3

Describing Data

Data often arrive in raw form, as long lists of numbers. In this case your job is to summarize the data in a way that captures its essence and conveys its meaning. This can be done numerically, with measures such as the average and standard deviation, or graphically. At other times you find data already in summarized form; in this case you must understand what the summary is telling, *and what it is not telling*, and then interpret the information for your readers or viewers.

This chapter focuses on aspects of describing data: finding the center of the data, such as an average; describing how spread out the data are, its distribution; finding relationships between sets of data; and presenting data visually.

3.1. Averages

Central tendency is the formal expression for the notion of where data is centered, best understood by most readers as "average." There is no one way of measuring where data are centered, and different measures provide different insights. Here we discuss three such measures: the mean, median and mode.

Basic Measures of the Center

Average, Mean
The words *average* and *mean* are synonymous.

> To compute the mean of a list of numbers, first sum the list and then divide by the number of entries.

☞ A survey of five gas stations shows that regular unleaded gasoline is selling at the prices of $1.39, $1.43, $1.43, $1.45, $1.70. The mean is found by taking the sum of these prices, $7.40, and dividing by 5, to get $1.48.

Median

The median of a list of numbers is the middle value.

> To compute the median of a list of numbers, put the list in ascending order and find the entry in the middle. If there is an even number of entries, average the middle two values.

☞ There were five prices in the previous list: $1.39, $1.43, $1.43, $1.45, $1.70. The middle entry when taken in order is the third, $1.43, the median.

☞ If a sixth price was included on the list ($1.39, $1.43, $1.43, $1.45, $1.70, $1.72) the median would be the average of the middle two, $1.43 and $1.45, which is $1.44. Notice that the mean in this case jumps to 1.52 from 1.48.

Mode

Mode is a less-used measure. It represents the most common amount.

☞ In the list $1.39, $1.43, $1.43, $1.45, $1.50, $1.51, since $1.43 occurs twice, the mode is $1.43. If there are two different amounts on the list which share in being the most common, the list is called *bimodal*.

For small sets of data these numbers can easily be computed with the aid of a hand calculator. For larger data sets, Chapter 9 explains how to use Excel to carry out the computation. For the largest data sets, for instance those that come up in computing the average salary of all U.S. workers, the average is estimated, as described in Chapter 4.

Combining and Comparing Averages

How to combine averages. Combine averages with care.

> To compute an average of a set of numbers that are divided into two (or more) smaller lists, do not compute the average of the lists separately and then take the average of those averages.

☞ On a lake two types of fish are caught, bass and trout. The average weight of the bass that are caught is 3 pounds. The average weight of the trout is 1 pound. You cannot conclude that the average weight of fish caught in the lake is 2 pounds. That average depends on the number of each kind of fish that is caught, not just the weight.

> If one list has m entries and an average value of M and another list has n entries and an average of N, the average overall is $\frac{mM+nN}{m+n}$.

☞ Suppose that 90 bass are caught with an average weight of 3 pounds and 30 trout are caught with an average weight of 1 pound. The average weight of all fish caught is $\frac{90\cdot3+30\cdot1}{90+30} = 2.5$ pounds.

Cautions about combining groups: apples and oranges. In computing an average, be careful about combining groups in which the average for each group is of more interest than the overall average. For instance, in investigating the increase in the average weight of football players, you are probably more interested in separate groups, such as linemen, than the overall average. If you combine the groups, then an overall change

33

in the average might be due to the change in the number of members in a subgroup.

> Avoid combining distinct quantities in a single average.

If this warning is ignored, paradoxical results can appear.

☞ A football team has a defensive roster with 10 linemen, each 300 pounds, and 8 backs, each 200 pounds. The overall average weight works out to be 256 pounds. Three more linemen are added, each weighing 290 pounds and one back has been added, weighing 195 pounds. The average weight works out to be 258. Hence, the overall average has gone up although in each category it has gone down.

☞ Hoss and Little Joe eat out at the restaurants FastAndGreasy and GourmetTouch. On his visits to FastAndGreasy, Hoss spends more on average than does Little Joe; similarly, on his visits to GourmetTouch he spends more on average than does Little Joe. Yet overall Hoss has a smaller restaurant bills than does Little Joe. How can this be? This is because Hoss visits FastAndGreasy most of the time, where the cost is much lower than at GourmetTouch, and this brings his overall average down, whereas Little Joe usually visits GourmetTouch, bringing his overall average up.

For further illustration, here are a couple of other situations in which you would have to watch out for combinations of group leading to paradoxical behavior of averages.

- In comparing the average delay for different airlines, compare the averages for each airport separately; otherwise the airlines that mostly fly to good-weather airports will come out ahead.
- In comparing the average salary of graduates of different colleges, compare the average for each major separately. Otherwise a school with many engineering majors will probably come out ahead of the school with more teaching majors, even though in each category (engineering and teaching) the other school might come out ahead.

Comparing the Mean and the Median

Often the mean and median will be quite close, but not always. Especially in cases when they differ markedly, a more detailed examination of the data is usually needed, and when one but not the other is given, caution is called for.

> The mean is greatly affected by large variations in individual numbers in a data set, whereas the median is not.

☞ If BigComputerCorp gives giant raises to its board of directors, the average salary for all workers may go up considerably; the median will be unchanged.

☞ In 1999 the Gallup Poll of Christmas shopping revealed that, as compared to 1998, the average expenditure for Christmas purchases had increased considerably, but the median of expenditures had fallen. How is this possible? One likely explanation was that the most well-to-do individuals were spending vastly more on presents, thus pushing the average up, but that at the same time most shoppers were spending less, thus lowering the median expenditure.

In this last example, if the interest is on the impact of Christmas sales on the economy, the mean is probably more important; however, if the interest is on the economic status of the typical American family, the median is probably more revealing.

Warning: Average versus Typical

We will go into this in greater detail in Chapter 8, but we want to discuss our earlier warning in more detail here.

☞ In 2002 the team roster for the Minnesota Vikings revealed that the average weight of a player was 249 pounds. Yet out of the 62 players on the roster, only two weighed within 5 pounds of that amount. In fact, weights in that range were far from typical.

What's going on here? Football teams usually have a large number of players below 220 (23 for the Vikings) and a lot of players above 280 (18 for the Vikings). These two groups tend to cancel each other out in computing the average, yielding an average of around 250, although few players weigh around that weight.

Similarly, the median tends to fall in a range that is between the two groups, and it doesn't represent a "typical" player in any sense either.

There is a joke that the typically American woman gives birth to 2.1 children in her lifetime. The fact is, 2.1 is the average, but certainly there are no women who give birth to a fractional number of children.

✎ Whenever you see a press release or hear a statement involving a median, try to find out more about the amounts, especially the highest amounts and the lowest amounts. Because the median is simply the value at the middle of a ranked group, it cannot tell you anything about how spread apart the members of the group are. For example, the governor's eight closest advisers could be averaging $200,000 each in salary, but because there are also dozens and dozens of low-paid clerks and housekeepers on the governor's staff, the median salary for the governor's staff may be quite modest. The median is simply the salary of the person who is ranked at the middle of the staff salaries. If the governor's press secretary announces only the median, the boss looks like a frugal manager who is not granting any monetary favors to his close advisers.

There are times, as well, when a source wants to emphasize the mean and steer clear of the median. For example, a school district may have a large number of pupils scoring at the lowest levels of a standardized test. But because the district has one pocket of extraordinarily high-achieving pupils, the mean test score for the district may be somewhat respectable. The median would probably produce a much lower score than the mean, and a look at the entire data set would reveal the large number of pupils at the bottom of the state's barrel.

3.2. Variation

The average and median give an indication of how data are centered, but it is often important to present a picture of how the data are spread out. For instance, in two companies the average clerical salary might be $30,000, but in one company the range might be from $25,000 to $40,000 (with most in the lower range to bring the average down) and in the other the range might be from $20,000 to $32,000 (with most in the upper range, to bring the average up). Which company would an ambitious clerk rather work for?

There is a variety of measures used to describe the variation or distribution of data. In research reports you will often see the variation described in one of these three ways: standard deviation, quartiles and percentiles.

Standard Deviation

Roughly stated, the *standard deviation* gives the average of the differences between the numbers on the list and the mean of that list. If data are very spread out, the standard deviation will be large. If the data are concentrated near the mean, the standard deviation will be small. The formula for computing the standard deviation is complicated, but calculators and spreadsheets such as Excel (see Chapter 9) can quickly perform the computation.

> Use Excel or a calculator's built-in commands to compute the standard deviation.

On a calculator you may see the standard deviation denoted in a number of ways. Common symbols include: σ, s, s_n, s_{n-1}, σ_n, and σ_{n-1}. These symbols represent slightly different but closely related quantities. As long as the number of elements in the list, n, is fairly large, say greater than 20, computations of each of these will yield roughly the same value.

Quartiles

Sometimes it helps to rank-order the data and then divide it into fourths. The dividing line between the lowest fourth and the rest of the data is called the *first quartile*. The second quartile divides the lower two fourths from the upper two fourths;

that is, the second quartile is the same as the median, the dividing line between the lower half and the upper half. The third quartile divides the upper quarter of the group from the rest.

> The quartiles divide the ordered data into four parts. The first quartile splits off the lowest fourth and the third quartile divides off the top fourth.

☞ If 10,000 students take a standardized test, the first quartile is the score that separates the lowest 2,500 student scores from the rest. So, the score that is 2,500 from the bottom can serve as the first quartile. If a group is small, so that it is not clear where the cut off should be, it is best not to use quartiles. (For instance, with a group of six it is not clear if the first quartile should identify the lowest student or the lowest two students; you wouldn't use quartiles in this setting. But with 106 students, if you use a cutoff that separates the lowest 26 or 27 students it doesn't matter; the result will almost always come out about the same.)

Percentiles

In a very large group, rather than divide it into quarters using the quartiles, it is often more useful to divide it into hundredths, using percentiles. This finer subdivision permits a more detailed description of the data.

☞ Again, suppose that 10,000 students take a standardized test. The first percentile represents the score that 100 students scored beneath, since one percent of 10,000 is 100. Similarly, 2,000 students scored beneath the twentieth percentile. The top 500 students are those who scored above the 95th percentile. Notice: The 25th percentile is the first quartile, and the 50th percentile is the median score.

☞ If a score is at the 90 percentile, it means that roughly 90 percent of scores were below that score and 10 percent were above. Similarly, if a score is at the 99 percentile, roughly 99 percent of scores were lower.

Interpreting the Standard Deviation

Here are two basic rules of thumb.

> 67 percent of the group is within 1 standard deviation of the mean.

> 95 percent of the group is within 2 standard deviations of the mean.

That is, about two-thirds of the data are within one standard deviation of the mean and about 95 percent of the data are within two standard deviations from the mean.

☞ If the average clerical salary at a company is $30,000 with a standard deviation of $5,000, a rough estimate is that two thirds of the clerical employees make between $25,000 and $35,000 and 95 percent make between $20,000 and $40,000.

↘ This rule applies best when the group is large, say at least 60. It also applies best when the data are spread out "normally;" see Chapter 7 for more about the Normal Distribution. When the data are spread out very irregularly, perhaps occurring in bunches, the rule does not apply as well.

✎ "Standard deviation" is not a term reporters should be using often in their copy, but it is a useful concept in understanding a set of data, especially understanding how "spread out" the results are. For example, two towns could each have average household incomes of $80,000 a year, but if you then discover that the first town's standard deviation is $6,000 and the second town's standard deviation is $28,000, you've just learned something important about these two towns. In the first town, 95 percent — nearly all the households — earn between $68,000 and $92,000 (two standard deviations from the average), which is an incredibly homogeneous group of families. In the second town, by contrast, 95 percent of the households earn anywhere from $24,000 a year to $136,000. Expect to find substantial wealthy neighborhoods, and substantial low-income neighborhoods, in the second town — but not in the first.

3.3. Correlation

Sometimes you see data measuring two different things. Examples might include the height and weight of each player on
a football team, or the expenditure of each of a state's school
districts and the average SAT score for each district. The question then arises: Are the two quantities related? Sometimes a
scatterplot can help; here is one in which each dot represents
a student in a statistics course. The horizontal scale measures
the student's midterm score; the vertical scale measures her
final exam score. The added line, the "trendline" is the line
that best fits the data. (In Chapter 9 we will summarize how to
use Excel to construct diagrams. In brief, after selecting two
columns of data and having Excel build the scatterplot, there
is a chart option to add the trendline.)

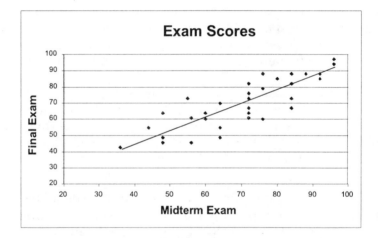

FIGURE 1. Scatterplot with r close to 1.

Such plots can be revealing but often are not practical.
There is a numerical measure of the connection, called the
correlation coefficient, usually denoted with the letter r. (A
related measure is the *coefficient of determination*, r^2; it will
be discussed again in detail in Chapter 5.)

> The correlation coefficient tells you if the data
> all lie close to a line.

In the previous diagram the data points are close to the line, so the value of r is close to 1. The actual computation, which we don't give here, shows that r is actually .82. In the next figure the data is much more scattered, and r turns out to be only .26.

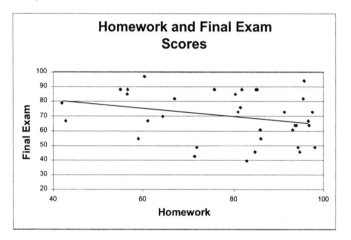

FIGURE 2. Scatterplot with r close to 0.

Compute r using Excel, as described in Chapter 9.

Here are the basics of interpreting the Correlation coefficient.

(1) The value of r is always between -1 and 1. If r is close to 0, then there appears to be little linear relationship between the two quantities.

☞ Suppose that in a certain course it is found that the correlation between the students' first exam scores and final course totals is .2, but the correlation between the first homework project score and the final course total is .8. Then an advisor should feel more confident using the project grade to assess a student's prospects in the course than using the exam score.

(2) If the correlation is positive, $r > 0$, then in general the two quantities increase in unison. See Chapter 5 for more information about drawing conclusions from your data.

☞ Since adult male height and weight have a positive cor-relation, if you know that Tom is taller than Jim, you might bet that Tom is heavier than Jim too. In situations for which r is positive but close to 0, the probability of your winning the bet are not much more than 50%. If r is close to 1, you can feel more confident in winning the bet.

(3) When r is negative there is said to be a negative correlation. If one quantity increases, the other tends to decrease.

☞ There is a negative correlation between the amount of time a woman exercises and her resting pulse. People who exercise more tend to have lower heart rates. If one woman exercises much more than another, you can guess that her resting pulse rate will be lower. Again, your confidence in this guess depends on whether r is closer to -1 or to 0.

(4) *Don't confuse correlation for causation.* It is true that men's weight and height are (highly) positively correlated, but that does not mean that by gaining weight you will become taller.

(5) The group from which the correlation is computed must be understood in interpreting the correlation. For exam-ple, studies have shown that the correlation between SAT scores and college grades is close to 0, but this is computed for all college students in the country. At a given university the admissions policy should more likely consider if there is a positive correlation between SAT scores and perfor-mance among students at that university. Here's another example to illustrate the point.

☞ A group of students is given a strength test, and two months later given the same test again. You would expect to find a strong correlation between the results; students who were stronger in September will still be stronger in November. However, if those students who scored in the lower range on the first test were given special training for the intervening two months, the level of correlation would be greatly reduced.

✎ Reporters first encountering the coefficient r in a research report usually find the rascal's interpretation to be counterin-tuitive. That's because an extremely low negative decimal can signal an extremely strong association between two factors.

Let's say the state board of education wanted to look for any relationship between each school district's scores on standardized tests and (a) the amount each district spends per pupil on education, (b) the number of violent crimes per capita reported in each (district's) community each year, and (c) the percentage of male teachers in each district. The correlation between test scores and violent crimes was $r = -.59$, the correlation between test scores and male teachers was $r = .01$, and the correlation between test scores and spending per pupil was $r = +.53$. The -.59 seems the smallest amount, but it represents the strongest relationship of the three, because it's farthest from zero. The negative sign simply signals the direction of the relationship — that is, the larger the number of crimes per capita, the lower the test scores tend to be in a district. But when an r is close to zero, then the study found no pattern of association — that is, the gender of the teachers seems to have no connection with test scores. The positive sign for the r for per-pupil spending (+.53) indicates that the two factors vary together: whenever you see high spending per pupil, you're likely to see high test scores.

How close to 0 must r be before you declare "no correlation"? That depends on a few additional factors, which we'll discuss in Chapter 5.

3.4. Interpreting Tables

Most research results don't stop at the reporting of one characteristic for the entire group. Things get interesting when researchers can measure that characteristic more specifically and then compare the results for various subgroups. The results are usually summarized efficiently in tables, which researchers sometimes call "crosstabs."

Male	Female	Total
638	368	1006

TABLE 1. A Basic Crosstab

Let's take a simple example. In 1997 the American Society of Newspaper Editors conducted a random-sample survey of about 1,000 newspaper journalists across the country. The

43

survey found that 638 journalists were male, and 368 were female. A crosstab table reporting the results would look as in Table 1.

As we discuss in more detail in Chapter 10, percentages often make more sense to more readers than raw numbers do, because they put the numbers into context. Often the researchers provide the percentages in the table, as in Table 2.

That was interesting enough (especially considering that the percentage of women was 35 percent 10 years earlier, so the proportion of women didn't change much in the '90s). But

	Male	Female	Total
Number	638	368	1006
Percentage	63%	37%	100%

TABLE 2. A Crosstab with Percentages

the researchers then wondered if the gender breakdown is different for different age groups. Because they asked the age of every journalist in the survey, they were able to create three categories of age: under 30, 31–50, and over 50. The crosstab looked like Table 3.

	Male	Female	Total
Under-30	95	96	191
31–50	445	244	689
Over-50	98	28	126
Total	638	368	1006

TABLE 3. A Crosstab with Categories and Totals

In the language of crosstab tables, a "row" always runs horizontally, and a "column" always runs vertically.

Notice that there's now a column for "total" at the right and a row for "total" at the bottom, and their contents are different. The column on the right has totaled up the under-30s across their row, the 31–50 group across its row, and the over-50s across their row. The total at the bottom of the table has totaled up the male column and then the female column. And both the "total" row at the bottom and the "total" column at the right should add up to 1,006, the entire number of people in the survey. The two have just reached 1,006 in two different ways.

	Male	Female	Total
Under–30	95	96	191
	50%	**50%**	**100%**
31–50	445	244	689
	64%	**35%**	**100%**
Over–50	98	28	126
	78%	**22%**	**100%**
Total	638	368	1006
	63%	**37%**	**100%**

TABLE 4. A Crosstab with Totals and Percentages

The curious reporter senses that there may be another story (or as the statistician would put it, another "significant difference") in this crosstab. Could the proportion of women be greater among the young journalists than among the older journalists? A table with percentages will make things more obvious. Computing the male-female percentages for each of the three age groups yields Table 4.

Now it becomes a little clearer that women are relatively rare in the over-50 age group (22 percent), and that among journalists under 30 you're just as likely to find a female (50%) as a male (50%). The age group in the middle (31–50 years old) shows a percentage of women (35%) about halfway between the two age groups on the ends.

Notice how anyone trying to add up all the percentages under "male" in Table 4 would get far more than 100 percent, which wouldn't make sense. These percentages are understood to be "percentages within the age group at the left," or "percentage within row," so it would only make sense to add the percentages across a given row.

But sometimes the table contains so much percentage-information that it can get confusing, as in Table 5.

	Male	Female	Total
Under-30	95	96	191
% within row	**50%**	**50%**	**100%**
% within column	**15%**	**26%**	**19%**
31–50	445	244	689
% within row	**65%**	**35%**	**100%**
% within column	**70%**	**66%**	**69%**
Over-50	98	28	126
% within row	**78%**	**22%**	**100%**
% within column	**15 %**	**8%**	**13%**
Total	638	368	1006
% within row	**63%**	**7%**	**100%**
% within column	**100%**	**100%**	**100%**

TABLE 5. A Crosstab with Row and Column Percentages

Table 5 tells us that 15 percent of the male journalists are under 30, and that 26 percent of the female journalists are under 30. That's what's meant by "% within column," the second set of percentages given in each box. This time, if we add up the "second percentages" in each box all the way down the column, they should indeed add up to 100 percent. Note also that the "second percentages" in the far-right "total" column are not 100 percent. This means that 19 percent of all newspaper journalists, regardless of gender, are under 30, that 69 percent are between 30 and 50, and so on. In this case, we "found the story" in the percentages within row, that is, that the proportion of women among young journalists is much higher than the proportion of women among older journalists. In other situations, the story may be found in the percentages within column. To guard against missing the story, simply be aware of important differences among the subgroups horizontally, and among the subgroups vertically as well.

It's important to know how to interpret a contingency table, but presenting a contingency table in a graphic is risky business. That's because most readers or viewers will find it difficult to grasp two or three breakdowns of different factors without some careful examination. Still, tables are useful additions to many stories, as long as they're kept simple. Tables can quickly summarize rankings, poll results or sports standings; they can compare features, fees, attendance or other numerical data; they can show changes over time — all without calling in the graphics department. But because a table is a collection of boxes with numbers, it shouldn't overwhelm its readers with numbers.

3.5. Displaying Data with Graphs

The are many styles of graphics used to display data. Three common ones are the pie chart, the bar chart, and the line graph. Each is particularly useful in certain situations, but there are basic errors and warnings that come with each one.

Pie Charts

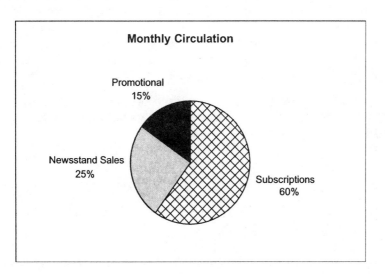

FIGURE 3. A Pie Chart.

Use a pie chart to illustrate how a group is divided up into *separate, distinct* parts.

☞ Use a pie chart only to indicate how a *single* collection is divided up into smaller parts. For instance, at BigCollege University students can be in one of three schools, Arts and Sciences, Business, or Education. Hence, a pie chart representing the group could be divided into four sections, one for each school and one for undeclared majors.

⋎ Make sure the categories are distinct. For instance, you wouldn't break up the set of automobiles sold into domestic, foreign and compact; these categories overlap. A good check for this is that the percentages of all the slices should add up to 100.

☞ This last point can be subtle; in the previous example of BigCollege what is to be done with students with double majors? One option would be to have students categorized by "first major." Another choice would be to count the total number of "majors" rather than the total number of students. In either case the sum of the percentages must come out to be 100. (There is another option if the total comes out to be slightly off from 100; that is include a comment like "the total exceeds 100 percent because of double majors." See Chapter 2 for dealing with errors arising from rounding.

⋎ Be sure that the slices are sized proportionally. If a slice represents 50 percent, then it should occupy exactly half the pie; similarly, 25 percent should be represented by a quarter of the pie.

⋎ Also, make sure the slices are shaded in a way that makes them clearly distinct and that they are labeled so that they are easily identified.

Bar Charts

☞ Bar Charts are called *Column Charts* in Excel.

⋎ Be sure you are measuring the same thing for each of the groups; that is, one bar shouldn't measure height and the next weight.

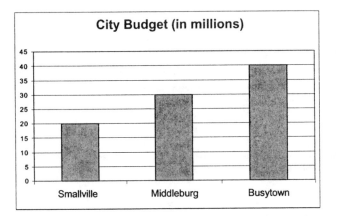

FIGURE 4. A Bar Chart.

Use a bar chart to show measurements of different groups.

☞ Have the heights of the bars consistent. The scale, usually on the left, should begin at 0. This way, if one bar represents a quantity that is twice as large as another, the corresponding bar is twice as high. The city budget chart above is recreated below using a different scale. Notice that with the new scale the difference between the budgets of Smallville and Middleburg is exaggerated.

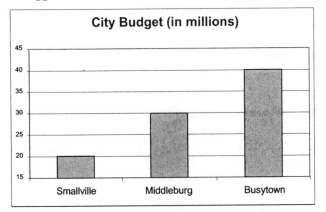

FIGURE 5. A Bar Chart with Skewed Scale.

☞ Make all the bars the same width; a bar that is both twice as tall and twice as wide as another has four times the area, an effect that can be very misleading. (If graphic images are used instead of bars, the same rule applies. Stack the images, rather than enlarging them in two dimensions.)

☞ Check the labeling.

Line Graphs

Line graphs are especially useful in illustrating something that is changing over time.

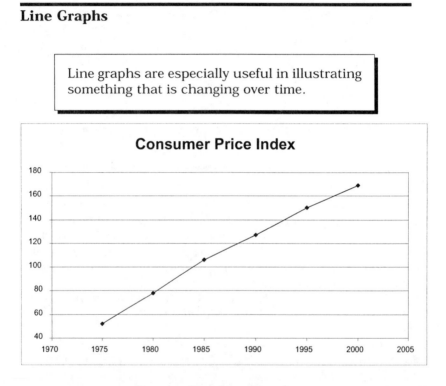

FIGURE 6. A Line Graph.

☞ As with bar charts, always try to have the scale (usually the left axis) begin at 0. If this is not feasible, make the adjustment obvious. If the bottom part of the scale is cut off, then small changes can appear significant.

☞ Be sure to have the base time scale evenly spaced. For example, the five equal units on the time scale should not read 1987, 1988, 1989, 1997, 1998.

4

Estimation

It is rare to have data on every single member of a large group. In making a prediction concerning an upcoming election, polling firms work with a relatively small sample of the voting population, often less than 1,000. In determining unemployment rates or income levels, the Bureau of Labor Statistics works with only a sample of the population. The best ways of attaining a sample are described in Chapter 6. Here we discuss how to move from a small set of information to an estimate of what a truly complete survey would reveal. We are now at the heart of inferential statistics.

In each case we will see that making the estimate is the easy part. The more difficult issue is measuring the reliability of the estimate.

Researchers usually take these four steps:

1. A subset, or *sample*, of a group of interest is surveyed. For example: A sample of 100 registered voters is surveyed and asked if they will vote for Smith; 56 respond yes. Methods of surveying are discussed in Chapter 6.
2. An estimate concerning the entire group of interest is formulated: 56 percent of voters will vote for Smith tomorrow.
3. The margin of error of the estimate is computed: the margin of error in this poll is ±10 percent with a confidence level of 95 percent. (We'll discuss the interpretation of this below.)
4. A conclusion is drawn. Based on this survey of voters, the election appears to be too close to call. (See Chapter 5.)

4.1. Polling Data: Estimating a Proportion

4.1.1. Estimating the population proportion

Estimating the proportion, or percentage, of a population with a certain property is a simple matter of computing percentages once a survey or sample has been taken.

☞ In a random telephone survey 56 out of 100 respondents say they will vote for Smith. Based on this, 56/100 = .56, or 56 percent, will vote for Smith.

4.1.2. Margin of Error and Confidence Intervals

An estimate of a population alone is not worth much. How confident should we be of the estimate? We need some sense of how good it is. A numerical measure of the quality of the estimate is usually given by the *margin of error.*

> Every estimate of a population proportion should come with a margin of error.

Interpreting Margin of Error and Confidence Level.
☞ A recent poll indicates that 59 percent of voters favor Smith in the coming election. The margin of error in the poll was ±10 percent with a confidence level of 95 percent.

This means that the pollster believes that the true percentage of voters who favor Smith lies between 49 and 69 percent. The techniques used in the poll will produce a result within that interval 95 percent of the time.

Computing the Margin of Error. Statistical theory provides formulas for estimating the margin of error. Here are two useful, basic rules of thumb. If a survey polls n individuals, we have:

> Margin of Error at 95 % confidence $\pm \dfrac{1}{\sqrt{n}}$

❖ 4.1. POLLING DATA ❖

> Margin of Error at 90 % confidence $\pm \frac{.8}{\sqrt{n}}$

☞ In the previous example there are 100 voters surveyed, so find the 95 percent confidence interval by computing that $\frac{1}{\sqrt{100}}$ = .1 or 10 percentage points.

☞ Similarly, find the 90 percent confidence interval by computing that $\frac{.8}{\sqrt{100}}$ = .08 or 8 percentage points.

The Confidence Interval. Rather than refer to the margin of error, statisticians often use the *confidence interval.*

> If the estimate is E and the margin of error is m, the confidence interval is from $E - m$ to $E + m$.

☞ If a the poll gives 59 percent with a margin of error of 10 percent, the confidence interval is the range from 49 percent to 69 percent, with 95 percent confidence.

☞ For the same example, the 90 percent confidence interval with be the range from 51 percent to 67 percent.

Interpreting the Confidence Interval. It is unlikely that a sample of only 100 voters will yield a very accurate estimate of the population proportion. The meaning of a 95 percent confidence interval is that with this method of estimating the percentage, using a sample of this size, the estimate will be within 10 percentage points of the true value 95 percent of the time; the remaining five percent of the time (or about 1 out of 20 times) these polling methods and sample size will yield a result that misses the true value by more than 10 percent.

Notice that in the previous example, you can say with 90 percent confidence that a majority of voters favor Smith, but at 95 percent confidence, the level you should be working at, you can't make that claim.

Which confidence level should be used? In general, professional surveys use a 95 percent confidence interval. If no confidence level is given for polling data you can assume it is 95 percent. By using a lower confidence level the researcher can claim a smaller margin of error, but this occurs at the expense of having surveys turn out to be inaccurate more often. In situations in which errors are more costly, a higher level of confidence is called for: In medical testing and other critical areas, a confidence level of 99 percent or even 99.5 percent is usually used. This is discussed more in chapters 5 and 7 where hypothesis testing is described.

↰ Surveys can be beset by all kinds of errors. In general, surveys that are not conducted by professional poll takers should be labeled as *"nonscientific."*

✎ Most news organizations agree that every story on a survey or poll should give the dates of the interviewing, state who sponsored the survey, state the size of the sample and give the margin of error.

It's difficult enough just understanding the confidence level yourself, but how do you convey it to readers? For most audiences, this level of detail should suffice:

> In a survey conducted last week by XYZ News, nearly 59 percent of the county residents polled said they favored the ban on development in the wetlands ... The survey contacted 400 residents, for a margin of error of plus or minus 5 percentage points. Now comes the stickier part. The margin of error is based on a confidence level of 95 percent, which means that if the same poll had been taken randomly in the county 100 times that day instead of just once, the result would have been within 5 percent of the correct percentage in 95 of the 100 surveys.

Too much? Here's a shorter way of explaining it: "The margin of error is based on a confidence level of 95 percent, which means there is only a 5 percent chance that the true percentage of all county residents favoring the ban is either below 54 percent or above 64 percent."

Another way: "The margin of error is based on a confidence level of 95 percent, which means there is a 5 percent chance that the figure is far off because randomness led to an erroneous estimate."

Table 1 summarizes of the margins of errors for some common sample sizes (all assuming random-sampling methods). For more values, use the rule of thumb given earlier: for a sample size of n, the margin of error with a 95% confidence level is approximately $1/\sqrt{n}$.

Sample Size	Margin of Error (95% Confidence Level)
50	±13.9 Percentage Points
100	±9.8 Percentage Points
200	±6.9 Percentage Points
300	±5.7 Percentage Points
400	±4.9 Percentage Points
500	±4.4 Percentage Points
750	±3.6 Percentage Points
1,000	±3.1 Percentage Points
2,000	±2.2 Percentage Points

TABLE 1. Margin of Error Table

4.2. Estimating a Mean

4.2.1. Basic Estimate for the Mean

Perhaps the second most common sort of quantity that needs to be estimated is the mean or average of some population: What is the average weight of an adult male? What is the average price of gasoline in our community? What is the average distance workers commute to work? Here the method for estimating the mean is simple: randomly sample the population and take the average of that sample.

☞ Fifty shoppers at a market are observed to have purchases totaling $2,700; a division quickly gives that the average purchase is $54.

Measuring the accuracy of this estimate is where statistics comes in.

4.2.2. Errors in the Estimate

Margin of Error. The formula for computing the margin of error is similar to that used when considering the population proportion:

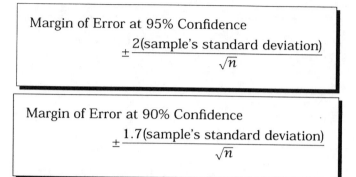

The quantity in the numerator, "sample standard deviation" was described in Chapter 3, and in Chapter 9 we explain how to compute it using Excel.

✘ Use this formula only with samples of size at least 30. If the sample size is less than 30, it is more difficult to correctly judge the accuracy of an estimate.

☞ In the case of the shoppers mentioned above, the mean was found to be $54. Suppose that the standard deviation in the amounts of their purchases was found to be $20. Then the above formula says that the 95 percent margin of error is

$$\frac{2(20)}{\sqrt{50}} = \pm\$5.66.$$

Interpreting the Margin of Error.

☞ A survey of 50 shoppers shows they have average purchase is $54, with an error of $\pm\$5.66$ with 95 percent confidence.

This means that the actual average purchase size is within $5.66 of $54; that is, after rounding, the actual average is predicted to be between $48 and $60. Predictions of a range of this sort will be correct 95 percent of the time, assuming that proper surveying methods have been applied.

Confidence Interval. As with polling data, statisticians will often refer to the confidence interval rather than the margin of error.

☞ In the previous example, rather than say that the average is $54 with a margin of error of $6, the result might instead say that the 95 percent confidence interval is the range of $48 to $60.

❖ 4.2. ESTIMATING A MEAN ❖

⋏ The same cautions that apply to estimating a population proportion apply in estimating a population mean: do not work with samples of less than 30, and be sure that the sampling is random, as described in Chapter 6. Again, unless a professional pollster is used, it is best to label such results as "nonscientific."

✎ Some reporters have some trouble seeing how "estimation of the mean" can be relevant to reporting situations. Yet time and again whenever complicated data appear, such estimates can be the key to summarizing complex data in a compact way. Here's a list of published stories that represents only a fraction of the tip of the iceberg:

- Taking a random sample of temperatures, to determine the average heat on a summer's day over the last 10 years.
- Taking a random sample of response times of emergency medical teams in 18 different neighborhoods, to determine the average response time in each part of the city.
- Taking a random sample of hotel rates in eight different cities, to determine which is the most expensive and which is the least expensive city in which to spend a night.
- Taking a random sample of the weights of interior linemen on Division I football teams in three different years, to determine whether college linemen are getting heavier.
- Taking a random sample of the length of customers' waits for their orders at various fast-food outlets, to determine which fast-food joint serves food the fastest.
- Taking a random sample of the arrival times of commercial flights, to determine which airline has the best "on-time" record.
- Taking a random sample of the gas-pump prices in different regions of the state, to determine whether gasoline prices are uniform throughout.
- Taking a random sample of local college students to determine the average amount of money students spend in town per week.

4.3. **Other Estimates**

In addition to estimating population proportions and averages, there are other measures of a group that sometimes must be measured. In Chapter 7 we'll discuss these in greater detail. Here we briefly mention three of them.

Difference of percentages. One week a poll says that Smith is favored by 54 percent of the voters with a margin of error of 4 percent. Two weeks later the poll says that he is favored by 46 percent of voters with a margin of error of 5 percent. Has his support gone down? It looks like it, but taking into account the size of the margin of error, it's not so clear. Answering the question depends on considering the difference, 54 - 46 = 8 and deciding if this is big enough to conclude that the difference is really positive. As discussed further in Chapter 7, combining the margins of errors is a bit tricky. Here's a basic rule of thumb:

> The margin of error in the difference of two estimates is at most 1.5 times the larger of the two margins of error.

☞ As in the previous example, in two surveys taken a week apart the support for Smith falls from 54 percent to 46 percent. The margin of error in the first survey is 4 percent and in the other it is 5 percent. The total margin of error is hence at most 1.5(5) = 7.5. Because the apparent drop is 8 percent, this exceeds the margin of error and you can conclude that the support for Smith has indeed decreased. (Note, you cannot conclude that fewer than 50 percent support Smith, since 46 is within 5 percentage points of 50.)

Difference of means. Morel, a delectable mushroom, average 5 ounces in Owen County; those in Brown County average 4 ounces. Can you conclude that morels in Owen County are heavier than those in Brown County? This again depends on the margin of error in each measure and how you combine them. See Chapter 7 for more on this topic.

Standard Deviation. Sometimes you need to estimate the amount of variation in a group, not just its average. For instance, it is not enough to know that pills produced by a drug manufacturer have an average weight as advertised; it is as important to know that the pills all weigh close to the average and do not vary in weight very much. See Chapter 7 for more on this.

When is a difference not a difference? In the view of the statistician, it's not a difference unless it exceeds the margin of error. Remember, these measurements based on polls or random samplings are merely estimates, and with every estimate comes a margin of error. But when the difference does not exceed the margin of error, that doesn't mean there's no news or no story here. It just means you have to be careful in explaining the difference.

Extending the example above with candidate Smith's drop in the polls, how would a reporter write the story if the candidate's support had slipped from 54 percent only to 49 percent? The difference is now only 5 percentage points, and that's not enough to cover the margin of error (7.5 percentage points). Some possible language:

- Smith appears to be holding on to about half the voter support in the race. While his percentage of support in the poll has slipped, the slip is not statistically significant.
- Smith's support may seem to have slipped, but it's unclear from this sample whether the apparent decrease is due to chance or a true slip in support.
- Smith's drop in support is not statistically significant; with a margin of error of 7.5 percentage points, the drop is so small that we cannot conclude that his support is actually falling.

Note that in none of these examples are the confidence levels given for the estimate of the differences. Unless the readership is obviously sophisticated in statistics, that level of detail will do more harm than good.

chapter

5

Inference: Drawing Conclusions from Data

The ultimate goal in collecting and analyzing data is to use it to draw conclusions: Which candidate is going to win the election? How should a candidate revise his campaign strategy to regain a lead? Is a tax change going to increase revenues? What starting lineup will lead to a winning basketball team?

What we are discussing here is called inference: What can we infer from the given data? This issue is already implicit in the discussion of polling data, estimating both a population proportion, and *the accuracy of that estimate.* Here we look more closely at inference.

5.1. Hypothesis Testing and p–Values

From estimate to inference

The basic idea of going from an estimate to an inference is simple. Drawing the conclusion with confidence, and measuring the level of confidence, is where the hard work of professional statistics comes in. First, a few examples will give the idea of inference.

☞ **Estimate:** This week's poll shows that Smith is supported by 54 percent of the voters; last week 48 percent supported him. **Inference:** Smith's support has increased.

☞ **Estimate:** 20 percent of people taking drug *A* improve, and 4 percent of people taking a placebo improve. **Inference:** Drug *A* helps patients.

The general setup for these situations falls under the name *hypothesis testing*. There is a hypothesis, or inference, that an investigator wants to make, and a statistical study is under-taken to determine whether that inference is correct. We will get into more of the details of hypothesis testing in Chapter 7 and will focus now on one important aspect of the process, the "*p*-value."

Confidence, *p*-values

Statistical inferences should come with a *p*-value, a numeri-cal measure of the confidence one has in the correctness, or reliability, of the conclusion. Here are some guidelines.

> In social science work, a *p*-value should be at most .05.

> In medical testing or criminal investigations, a *p*-value should be at most .005.

Traditionally, *p*-values are given in decimal form, not as percentages.

✎ As important as the *p*-value is, it rarely belongs in news copy intended for a general audience. Most reporters, however, will occasionally come upon the term in their source material, for example:

• A press release on a political poll might declare that if the election were held today Smith would win, and that the *p*-value of the results is .05.

• A company reporting laboratory results testing a new prod-uct might say that its drug has been shown to reduce facial wrinkles, with a *p*-value of .005.

• In documents from expert witnesses in a criminal trial, you may see that DNA test shows that the defendant was at the scene of the crime, and that the *p*-value of the DNA test was .005.

• Just keep in mind that — unlike the confidence level described in Section 3.1 — the lower the *p*-value, the more powerful the statistic. And if you see any result with a *p*-value of more than .05, regard the results with high suspicion. At the very least, ask your source why the likelihood of research error or random coincidence is so high. Could it be that the research effort came up empty?

Interpreting the *p*-value

We'll go into this more when we describe some advanced statistics in Chapter 7, but here are two examples to illustrate the basic idea:

☞ It is suspected that a die is not fair, that the probability of throwing a six does not equal one sixth, as it should. To test this, the die is thrown 600 times and it comes up six only 80 times; if the die were fair, you would expect it to come up six roughly 100 times. not 100 as would be expected. Being so far off from 100, you might conclude that the die is not fair.

But wait. Maybe the die is fair and you got so few sixes just because of the randomness of tossing the die. Using methods learned in a statistics course, you can compute that for a fair die the probability of having the number of tosses resulting in six differing this much from the expected 100 is small; precisely .032, or 3 percent.

Here is the result in statistical language. An experiment suggests that the die is not fair. The *p*-value of the test is .032.

So, in this example, should you conclude that the die is not fair? That depends. If your decision is for small stakes, say you are considering spending a dollar to buy a better set of dice, then feel comfortable with your decision. With $p \le .05$ you can safely assume the die is not fair. If your decision is more critical — say you are a prosecutor deciding whether to charge the manufacturer with false advertising — then no, with *p* greater than .005 you aren't confident enough to go to trial.

☞ In a trial of a new drug it is seen that 20 percent of patients in the drug test improve with the use of the drug, while only 13 percent improve among those taking a placebo. The study concludes that the drug is effective, with a p–value of .2. Based on this the drug company will decide **not** to market the drug. If the company approved drugs using p–values as high as .2, they might find that as many as 20 percent of the drugs they marketed would ultimately be found to be ineffective, a rate far too high to be acceptable.

5.2. Correlation

In examining the relationship between two variables, for instance a worker's income and number of years on a job, if you have accurate data you can compute the correlation coefficient r as described in Chapter 3. But does the fact that the correlation coefficient is not zero imply that there truly is a correlation between the two quantities? And if you conclude that there is a correlation, what can you conclude about the relationship between the two quantities? There are really three important issues:

- If your data are based on sample, you are only estimating the correlation coefficient. How good an estimate is it?
- If you have confidence in your estimate in the correlation, what can you conclude about the mathematical relationship between the two quantities being considered?
- If you conclude that there is a strong mathematical correlation between the quantities, what practical conclusions can you draw?

We take these three on separately.

Is there a correlation?

If you have a complete set of data and if the arithmetic is done correctly, you find the correlation coefficient precisely. But if you are just using a sample of a large group of individuals, can you be sure that it accurately reflects the population as a whole? Assuming that good sampling techniques are applied, here are the results. We are using a p–value of .05 — that is, in cases that the correlation is trivial, $r = 0$, in only five percent of the cases the test will conclude that the correlation is nonzero.

For a sample of 10 individuals, if $|r| \geq .63$ you can conclude that there is a nontrivial (nonzero) correlation.

For a sample of 30 individuals, if $|r| \geq .36$ you can conclude that there is a nontrivial (nonzero) correlation.

For a sample of 100 individuals, if $|r| \geq .2$ you can conclude that there is a nontrivial (nonzero) correlation.

All that is being concluded here is that $r \neq 0$. For instance, if you sample 30 individuals and find $r = .5$ you can conclude that $r \neq 0$, but it is quite possible that $|r|$ is much smaller than .5.

To conclude that there is a *strong correlation*, say $|r| \geq .5$, you need to demand that your test shows a much larger correlation coefficient. There are no simple rules of thumb here, and advanced statistical techniques are required in this situation.

Mathematical Interpretation of Correlation

If a statistician does a study and finds that there is a correlation between two characteristics, what can be concluded? For instance, what is the meaning of $r = .6$ as opposed to $r = .8$? The mathematical interpretation is contained in the *coefficient of determination*, r^2.

Compute the coefficient of determination, r^2, by squaring the correlation coefficient.

The value of r^2 for two characteristics gives the percentage of variation in one quantity that is explained by the other.

☞ Suppose a study shows that the correlation coefficient between adult male weight and height is $r = .7$. Then $r^2 = .49$. This means that in studying the variation of individual heights, about 49 percent of the variation in height is explained by variation in weight.

☞ Suppose that the correlation between a student's high school GPA and college GPA is found to be $r = .3$. Then $r^2 = .09$. Hence, about 9 percent of the variation in college GPA is explained by the high school GPA; other factors explain the other 91 percent of the variation.

This last example points to an important distinction. It is possible that the survey that gave the $r = .3$ result is very well done and that with a great deal of certainty r is very close to .3. In particular we are absolutely convinced that $r \neq 0$; that is that there is a nontrivial correlation. However, the correlation coefficient of $r = .3$ is fairly small, giving a coefficient of determination of $r^2 = .09$. That is, the relationship is real, but only 10 percent of the college GPA is determined by high school GPA.

↘ As we discuss next, do not confuse one quantity "explaining" another with it causing another. *Correlation does not imply causation!*

Practical Conclusions: Correlation versus Causation

We cannot say it loudly enough or repeat it too often:

Correlation does NOT imply causation.

A section of Chapter 8 is devoted to the confusion over correlation and causation, but we discuss it briefly here.

☞ A survey finds a high correlation between the value of the cars people drive and their income. Not surprising. But only a fool would conclude that by buying an expensive car he will raise his income. The correlation is obvious, but the causation isn't there. Yet, this is just the sort of argument that appears constantly, usually in less obvious ways.

Suppose you measure two characteristics, A and B, about a group of people. For instance, A = weight and B = height, or A = IQ and B = SAT score, or A = age and B = education level. A study is done and it is found that the correlation coefficient is quite large, say r = .95. Why might this be true? Here are some possibilities:

☞ **A causes B:** If A is the amount of liquid drunk in a day and B is the amount of urine produced, the correlation is high, and drinking liquid does cause a greater production of urine.

☞ **B causes A:** If A is the number of hours the street lights are on and B is the number of hours between sunset and sunrise, there is a strong correlation. But having street lights on doesn't lead to longer nights (if the city disconnects the lights then nights don't become shorter); it is the other way around.

☞ **There is no causation between A and B:** The number of hours per day I use my air conditioner and the number of hours my neighbor uses her air conditioner are closely correlated, but my using my air conditioner does not cause my neighbor to use hers, or vice versa. The causative factor is a third, unmentioned, factor: the daily temperature.

A third factor, C, that explains a correlation between two others, A and B, is called a **confounding factor**. More on this in Chapter 8.

Prediction and Predictors

> If the correlation between A and B is high, we say that A is a good predictor of B.

With our standard example, we have that there is a high correlation between adult male weight and height. Again, that doesn't mean that becoming heavier is going to make you taller. However, it does mean that you can use a man's weight to help you *predict* his height. If two men are randomly selected and you learn that one is 150 pounds and the other is 250, the odds are fairly strong that the heavier man is also the taller. Of course you might be wrong, but this is a reasonable prediction.

☞ In my statistics course of 75 students, the correlation between the midterm exam and final exam scores was .63. That is, with $r^2 = .4$, the first exam score is a reasonable *predictor* for the final exam score, explaining 40 percent of the variation in final exam scores. Alternately, a careful examination of the actual data shows that if two students were selected at random, there was about a 33 percent chance that the one with the lower midterm score would have scored higher on the final.

Significance and Statistical Significance

The dual meaning of the word *significant* brings into focus the distinction between drawing a mathematical inference and practical inference from statistical results. Consider this sentence:

☞ A recent study shows that there is a statistically significant correlation between a student's height and GPA.

Perhaps this result was based on a very carefully done survey of a large number of students. The result that came out was that the correlation coefficient is $r = .05$. The surveyors have overwhelming evidence, say $p = .001$, that r is very close to .05, say $.04 \le r \le .06$. With a p-value of .001, this is *statistically significant*. We are certain that the correlation accurately describes the overall population.

But is this *significant* in the everyday meaning of the word? Well, $r = .05$ is a very small value. Squaring it to find the coefficient of determination yields $r^2 = .0025$. That is, though the correlation is real, only .25 percent of the variation of a student's gpa is explained by the student's height. Most of the variation of student gpa, 99.75 percent of the variation, is explained by other unknown variables. So, as a practical matter, the correlation is not very significant.

✎ It's unlikely any reporter will be writing lots of stories with details on correlation coefficients and p-values, but the basic relationships are quite common in research. If you see that a correlation coefficient is statistically significant, it's a good idea to describe the strength of the relationship — but also its weakness. For example, if a study finds that the correlation between baseball players' home runs and their RBI (runs batted in) is .40 and that it's statistically significant, then you can conclude that "the more home runs a player hits, the higher his RBI total will be as well," or "The number of home runs generally predicts the RBI level as well."

But this is not an ironclad association. The coefficient r of .40 means that $r^2 = .16$, which means that the home run level explains only 16 percent of the variation in a player's RBI total — and that other factors explain the other 84 percent of the variation. You can't go into that detail in most news stories (especially not in sports stories), but you can at least acknowledge it by writing, "the more home runs a player hits the higher his RBI total will be, *although several other factors influence the RBI output as well.*"

5.3. Fallacy: Regression to the Mean

Although the "Regression to the Mean" fallacy occurs regularly, the idea of the fallacy is often misunderstood. Here are a few examples in which the regression to the mean fallacy could occur:

☞ A teacher compares student scores on a series of exams and notes that among the students scoring in the top 20 percent on the first exam, the scores on the second exam were much closer to the class mean. Similarly, among those scoring the worst on the first exam, the second exam scores fell closer to the mean.

☞ A medical tester gives a blood pressure medication to group of patients and observes that among those whose blood pressure tested the highest before the treatment, there was a significant lowering of blood pressure rates.

☞ Comparing baseball batting averages: for the group of players with the highest averages in one month, the following month their averages were much closer to the overall average among all players.

↘ In none of these cases can you conclude that the population overall is becoming more centralized.

In each of these examples, it is a misinterpretation of the data to conclude that over time everyone in the group is becoming more like the average. This misinterpretation is called the *Regression to the Mean* fallacy.

> Concluding that the population is becoming more centralized by observing behavior at the extremes is called the "Regression to the Mean" Fallacy.

The Explanation. If we concentrate only at the extremes of a population, it will always look as if there is, over time, a flow toward the mean. This is because some individuals were at the extreme not for some good reason, but just by chance; some students achieve high test scores by lucky guessing, some people had high blood pressure because we tested them on a particularly stressful day, and some batters had a high batting average because they faced unusually weak pitching. For these individuals, the follow-up test will have them again much closer to their natural ranking, near the mean, and thus they will pull the average of the entire extreme group toward the mean with them.

Note too that although this group of lucky ones is now pulling an average down in the follow-up, there will be a new group of lucky ones taking their place.

> When looking for a change in a population, do not look only at the extremes; there you will always find a motion to the mean. Look at the entire population.

☞ If you are interested in what is happening with individual weights, don't just look at the heaviest people. There you will detect a drop in average-weight. Some of them are successfully dieting, and this might show that weights in this group of this heavy group are moving down. Similarly, if you just study the lightest in the population you will note an upward drift of weights. But overall the distribution of weights in the population might not be changing. For every heavy individual who successfully diets, there might be an average weight individual who for some reason gains a large amount of weight.

Further discussion of Regression to the Mean appears in Chapter 8.

chapter

6

Surveying and Experimental Design

The most famous of statistical blunders was the unanimous declaration by the major polling organizations that Dewey was set to beat Truman in the 1948 presidential election. Truman's waving of the Chicago Tribune's **DEWEY WINS!** headline shamed the pollsters. That wake–up call led to an examination of surveying techniques. Today polls consistently, accurately predict the outcome of presidential elections, sampling as few as 1 out of every 20,000 voters.

Moving from the abstract mathematics of statistics to the real world of performing surveys and designing experiments to test hypotheses is a difficult step. We can't begin to present the necessary background to prepare you to become a statistical researcher. Our goal is to help you understand the risks of faulty techniques and to understand the results offered by the professional statistician and researcher.

6.1. Surveying Techniques

Designing your survey

There are rumors that the coach of a college basketball team might soon be fired. You want to find out what the campus thinks: what percent favor the coach, what percent want to see him leave? How do you go about surveying your population?

You may not be called on to produce such surveys, but understanding the basics of surveying might alert you to poorly done surveys, those that should come with the "nonscientific" disclaimer.

Select your sample randomly. Don't limit the group you survey to a particular location, or a particular time. Everyone in the total group that you are interested in should have an equal chance of participating in the survey.

Assure a high response rate. If you decide to call from a randomly generated phone list, maximize your response rate. If not, perhaps your survey will exclude a particular group (those who work evenings, for instance) whose responses might as a group differ markedly from those you do reach.

Don't depend on volunteered responses. Magazine surveys, in which readers are asked to mail in responses, or television surveys asking viewers to call in their opinions, can make for fun reading, but they shouldn't be taken as accurately reflecting any group. The group of people who are willing and interested enough to mail or call a response in might reflect far different attitudes than the "true" population as a whole.

Don't depend on an interpretation of respondents' answers. Asking a general question: What do you think should be done about the coach, and then categorizing the answer as a "fire" or "don't fire" response, requires so much interpretation that it introduces bias into the survey. Give the respondent clear choices. Discard ambiguous responses.

Don't ask questions that will produce ambiguous responses. For instance, asking people to respond to the statement "The mayor's salary is appropriate" will surely solicit answers that are difficult to interpret. Does a response of "I strongly disagree" mean that the responder believes the salary is too high or too low?

Check the randomness of your survey. If you know characteristics of your overall group of interest, compare them to the group your survey produced.

Say you know that 54 percent of registered voters are women. If your survey ended up including 75 percent women, something is probably wrong with your survey. Even if you are surveying concerning something for which you expect no connection between responses based on sex alone, the flaw in your survey puts into doubt any results you achieve. In addition to the sex of your respondents, you might consider income level, party of registration or education level. Any category for which there is reliable data on the population can be used as a check of the randomness of your survey.

Beware of the effect of question phrasing. Consider the two questions: "Do you support the decision to fire the basketball coach?" and "Do you support the university president's decision to fire the basketball coach?" Ostensibly they are asking the same question, but the different phrasings might lead some people to answer the questions differently. Sometimes such slight differences of phrasing can explain vastly different results obtained at the same time by different public opinion surveys.

There are no set rules for writing questions properly, but here are a few things to keep in mind.

- Be aware of the issue. When writing a question, do so in a way that does the least to shape a respondent's answers.
- In reading the results of surveys, find the original statements in the survey questions, so that you can be aware of biases the questions may have introduced.

Describing your survey

Here are a few guidelines if you perform your own survey.

Always state who conducted the survey. Even the best poll takers have troubles avoiding the pitfalls. Unless you are trained in statistical surveying techniques, do not suggest to your readers in any way that your results accurately reflect the population as a whole.

Give your reader a sense of the accuracy of your survey. Chapter 4 discusses how to measure the accuracy for a typical yes–no survey question: the margin of error is given by $\pm 1/\sqrt{\text{sample size}}$ (at a confidence level of .95). For example, if you randomly sample 50 people, the error is $\pm 1/\sqrt{50}$, or $\pm.14$, that is, about 14 percent.

6.2. Experimental Design

The results of scientific studies, especially in medicine, seem to be announced on a daily basis. Examples include everything from the effect of walking on life expectancy to the effect of vitamin C on common colds. Some of these studies are based on observing a population and thus are called *observation surveys*. Such studies can be reliable, but are fraught with dangers, especially from confounding factors; presentations of the results are plagued by the correlation–causation confusion. We'll talk about observational surveys in the next section.

Far better results are usually attained from an explicit experiment than from an observational study. For reasons from cost to ethics, it is not always possible to perform experiments, but well designed experiments can yield by far the most conclusive evidence.

You won't be designing or carrying out such experiments, but knowing the basics of experimental design will help keep you on alert when results are announced.

The language of experiment design

Treatment. Whether an experiment is testing the effect of a drug on a disease or the impact of decreasing classroom size on test scores, in technical presentations the word *treatment* is usually used. So, in the first example the treatment is the drug, in the second case the treatment is reduced class size.

Control Group. In a well designed experiment the subjects, whether medical patients or elementary school classes, must be broken up into two groups, the *treatment group*, which is to receive the treatment and a second group, the *control group*, that does not receive the treatment. Otherwise it will not be clear if changes in the population occur because of the treatment or because of some unseen factor. Having a control group permits the isolation of the treatment as the explanation for any observed changes in the treatment group.

Random Assignment. In setting up the treatment group and control group, the assignment *must* be at random; that is, each person has the same chance of being assigned to the first group as to the second group. For instance, if the two groups for a medical experiment are assigned by weight, it will not be clear if the observed changes are due to the drug, or somehow are caused by weight differences.

Placebo. Simply knowing that you're receiving a treatment, or not receiving a treatment, as a member of an experiment, can change the effect of a treatment. The *placebo effect* is the observation that, for instance, medical patients who believe that they are receiving treatment often improve, regardless of whether or not they really are receiving treatment. To address this, whenever possible a *placebo* is given to all members of the control group. This consists, in medical experiments, of a pill that looks identical to the treatment pill, but which does not contain a drug. This assures that no one in the group knows whether or not they are being treated.

Double Blind. Using placebos constitutes an effort to assure that the population is unaware of who is receiving treatment. But in a well designed experiment the caution goes a step further. It is assured that those administering the treatment and those measuring the results are also unaware of who is receiving treatment. This is the so–called *double blind*. There are two reasons for this. If the people applying the treatment know who is receiving the treatment and who is receiving the placebo, they may inadvertently communicate this information to the subjects. Second, knowing who has received the placebo and who hasn't might affect how one collects and interprets the information.

6.3. Observational Studies

Designing an experiment to test the effect of eating vegetables on longevity would be difficult, if not impossible. Could we possibly randomly select a group of people and dictate their diet to them over a period of, say 40 years, to see how it affected their life span? It is hard to imagine what could serve as a placebo in such an experiment. Similarly, designing an experiment to test the effect of classroom size on student learning would be extremely difficult and expensive.

In such cases there is no option other than to do observational studies. The most famous of these is the Nurse Health Study, actually two studies begun in 1976 and 1989. Each of these ongoing studies involves a population of over 100,000 women selected via mail–in surveys of women nurses. Each year or two follow–up surveys are conducted, both asking a range of questions, but also including taking, for instance, blood samples. These surveys have been used to study a large range of health issues, including the impact of diet, social factors, and the use of hormones, on health factors such as cancer and diabetes.

In doing this and similar studies, the scientists involved attempt to address the major problems associated with obser‑vational studies. One of these is that an effort is made to as‑sure a high response rate. For instance, in the original Nurse Health Study the original response rate was around 70 per‑cent (beginning with over 170,000 nurses) and in subsequent surveys the response rate has been about 90 percent.

More importantly, in drawing conclusions the researchers are careful to identify and adjust for confounding factors. For instance, it was recently found that a diet that includes whole grains lowers diabetes risk. But a number of lifestyle factors that are probably associated to diet habits that may confuse the picture. (For instance, do people who eat whole grains tend to exercise more, and if so, could it be the exercise and not the diet that affects diabetes risk?) By working with a large group and asking an extensive range of questions, such factors can be identified and adjusted for. Of course, doing so successfully is not a job for the amateur.

chapter

7

Advanced Statistics

7.1. The Normal Distribution

The Bell Shaped Curve

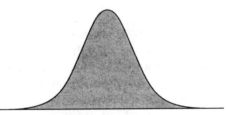

The *bell shaped curve* is well known. The term refers to any graph that resembles the one above in the following features.

1. The graph has a single high point, or maximum.
2. The graph is symmetrical around that maximum.
3. From the maximum the graph drops off to 0 in both directions, at first slowly, then dropping rapidly, and then leveling off as it approaches 0.
4. The maximum is located at the mean of the data set.

It turns out that graphs of this shape represent many commonly studied quantities. For instance, if one graphs the number of adult men in the United States of a given height, say computed to the nearest inch, the resulting graph will appear to be bell shaped. For this particular set of data the maximum is at 69 inches, 5 foot 9. Roughly 67 percent of the area under the graph occurs between 5 foot 6 inches and 6. That is, about two thirds of adult men have heights falling in that range.

On the other hand, other graphs definitely do not follow a bell shaped curve. If we considered all adult heights, not just men, the curve would have a double hump: One at 5 foot 9, corresponding to the average male height, and the other at 5 foot 4, the average of adult women in the United States.

There is a mathematical explanation as to why so many distributions, from heights and weights to standardized test scores, turn out to be bell shaped. We'll discuss that after looking at the *normal* curve and the *Central Limit Theorem*.

The Normal Curve

Here the advanced mathematics enters, so we will just mention the result very briefly. One particular bell shaped curve appears constantly in formal mathematical statistics. It is called the *normal curve*. It is the graph of the following function, which we include here only for completeness.

$$\frac{1}{\sqrt{2\pi}} e^{-x^2/2}$$

What is the point of having such a complicated formula? Well, despite being complicated, it is easily computed, especially with the aid of calculators and computers. Because of this, professional statisticians are able to calculate the answers to questions about any quantity that is closely related to the normal curve.

For instance, once we know that the adult male height is normally distributed with mean 69 inches and standard deviation 3 inches, tasks such as estimating the percentage of men over 6 foot 4 inches are easier to do.

Central Limit Theorem

The *Central Limit Theorem* is one of the most important concepts in statistics. An example will illustrate:

We've already noted that if you plot the height of all adults you get a curve that is not bell shaped; it has two humps. Imagine instead that you randomly pick two adults and take their average height and plot it. In the case that you pick two women you expect that average to be around 64 inches and if you pick two men you expect the average to be about 69. But if you pick one man and one women, the average will most likely be half way in between, around 66.5 inches. Since all the possibilities can occur, the graph will develop a new hump, at around 66.5 inches, and the other humps will be less pronounced.

Imagine now that you take a random sample of 100 adults and take their average height. Typically you will have about the same number of women as men, so that average will probably come out close to 66.5. If you keep repeating this process—randomly select 100 adults and compute their average height—and plot the results, the curve you get will resemble the normal curve very closely.

The central limit theorem makes this precise. It states that regardless of the shape of the curve of the original population, if you repeatedly randomly sample a large segment of your group of interest and take the average result, the set of averages will follow a normal curve.

A careful study of this theorem produces many of the results that have appeared earlier, such as in Chapter 5. For instance, our rubrics about using samples of at least 30 relate in part to a careful look at the meaning of the word *large* in the statement of the central limit theorem.

Why So Many Populations Distribute Normally

Consider the case of scores on a standardized test, say the mathematics SAT. If the test had only a few questions, we would not expect to see a normal curve. But with the large number of questions that appear on these tests, the overall score is determined by a mix of many factors, from the student's ability with a particular topic to the randomness of careless mistakes.

As another example, consider adult male height. If height were determined by a single gene or two, the distribution of heights would not be normal. But, in fact, there are many factors that determine height, from an array of genes to various nutritional factors.

In both these cases, SAT scores and height, the ultimate outcome depends on the combination of many factors. Once all these factors are combined (somewhat like averaging) the total outcome does appear normally distributed. In its formal statement the central limit theorem requires a *large* sample that is *random*. In these two examples the number of factors is large. However, they are not random. In the case of SAT scores, a student's ability with algebra is tied to her ability with geometry and her ability to avoid careless errors. In the case of heights, those with one gene favoring greater height tend to have several such genes. Because of this, the central limit theorem does not apply precisely, and understanding the inherent subtleties falls in the realm of advanced probability theory.

7.2. *z*–Scores

For most measurement there are a variety of units that can be used. A distance can be measured in terms of inches, feet, or meters, and so on. Hence, statistical estimates can be carried out in different units as well. For instance:

☞ The mean height of an adult male in the United States is 69 inches with a standard deviation of 3 inches. Or, the mean height of an adult male in the U.S. is 175 centimeters with a standard deviation of 7.6 centimeters.

In doing statistical work, it is convenient to convert to a unit of measurement in which the calculations are easily worked out. The idea is to use a system in which the population is distributed in a standard normal way, with mean 0 and standard deviation 1. In this system, the measure of an individual, called the *z–score*, indicates by how many standard deviations the individual differs from the mean of the entire group.

☞ Suppose a man is 6 foot 4 inches tall, 76 inches. This is 7 inches above the mean of 69. Since the standard deviation for heights is 3 inches, this man is 7/3 = 2.3 standard deviations above the mean. Hence, his *z*–score is 2.3 .

> For the normal distribution, *z*–scores above 2 or below -2 are fairly rare (happening about 5 percent of the time) and *z*–scores above 3 or below -3 are extremely rare, happening about .25 percent of the time.

(Our data on adult height has been rounded and the curve is not quite normal. More data of this sort are available on the Center for Disease Control web pages.)

7.3. Estimates

In Chapter 5 we discussed estimating a proportion of a population and also the mean of a population, for example, estimating the percentage of voters preferring candidate Smith, or the mean salary of a worker in a state.

In addition to estimating these two numbers, there are many other sorts of quantities that are estimated at times. Here are a few. Each comes with its own method of estimating the accuracy of the estimate (confidence intervals), but formulas are not given here.

Difference in Percentages

A poll one week announces that 48 percent of voters prefer Smith with a margin of error of 3 percent and with a confidence level of 95 percent. A week later the poll announces that Smith is now favored by 53 percent of voters, again with a margin of error of 3 percent at a confidence level of 95 percent. Do you conclude that Smith's support has gone up?

Initially your answer might be yes, it's gone from 48 to 53 percent, and that is an increase. But think again. With the given error on the first poll his support might have been as high as 51 percent, and at the time of the second poll his support might have been as low as 50 percent. Hence, maybe his support actually fell be 1 percent.

But think about it one more time. For the polls to make the real drop of 1 percent appear as an increase of 5 percent, both polls would have had to have been off near their extreme margin of error, with the errors in opposite directions. That seems pretty unlikely.

What we are considering here in general is using two estimates of population proportions to approximate the difference of the actual population proportions. Of course, estimating the difference is easy, but finding the margin of error is quite complicated. However, in a special case of polls using similar sample sizes and confidence levels, the margin of error is easier to compute.

81

> If two polls use similar size samples and have the same margin of error, the margin of error in the differences is given by multiplying the original margin of error by 1.5.

☞ In the case of the Smith polls mentioned above, both have margin of error 3 percent. Hence the margin of error in estimating the difference (still at the 95 percent confidence level) is 1.5(3) = 4.5. Because the estimate for the difference is 5 percent (53 − 48), which is greater than 4.5, we can conclude with a great deal of confidence that Smith's support has gone up, though not necessarily by 5 percent. In fact, we are only confident that the support has gone up by at least .5 percent.

The difference of means

☞ The average weight of a morel found in Owen County is 3.1 ounces whereas the average for Brown County is 2.5 ounces.

From this, can we conclude that on average Owen County morels weigh .6 ounces more than Brown County morels? The issues are similar to those just described for estimating the difference in population proportions. As the measures are estimates, each comes with a margin of error, so the difference between the two comes with a margin of error of its own.

In general there is no simple rule that gives a good measure for the margin of error in the estimation of the difference. But we do have this:

> If two means are estimated separately and the margin of errors are computed at the same confidence level, the margin of error for the difference is at most the sum of the two margin of errors.

In many situations the margin of error works out to be smaller than this sum, but identifying these situations calls on statistical methods beyond what we can present here.

This is critical when one is faced with the questions such as the one above, asking whether the morels of Owen County are actually larger on average than those of Brown County. If the confidence intervals are small, say .1 each, then this is probably the case. If the confidence intervals are large, say .5 ounces each, then the survey has done little to resolve the question.

Standard Deviation Estimates

At times the consistency of a quantity is as important as its actually value. For instance, it is not enough that pills produced by a manufacturer average 1 gram. It is as important that the weights of the pills are consistently 1 gram; if half the pills were 1.5 grams and the other half is .5 grams, the average would be 1 gram, but the variation is clearly too large.

Computing the standard deviation of the sample is described in Chapter 3. Estimating the error (or more precisely, finding the confidence interval) for this estimate of the standard deviation of the entire population, depends on fairly technical techniques, using the "Chi–Square" distribution. Here is a rough formula for the 95 percent confidence interval found using a sample of at least 30:

$$.8s \leq \sigma \leq 1.3s$$

In this formula, s denotes the standard deviation of the sample, and σ is the true standard deviation of the population.

☞ If 30 pills are randomly sampled and it is found that the mean weight of the pills is 1.01 grams with a standard deviation of .03 grams, then we let $s = .03$ in the formula and find that (with 95 percent confidence), the standard deviation of the weights of pills is somewhere between .024 and .039. Given this, and the fact (see Chapter 3) that 5 percent of results lie more than 2 standard deviation from the mean, it follows that possibly 5 percent of all pills manufactured fall outside of the range $[1.01 - 2(.039), 1.1 + 2(.039)] = [.93, 1.09]$.

7.4. Hypothesis Testing

The formal language of hypothesis testing is more than most journalists need to know. But embedded in this language are some key ideas that will help you in being alert to issues that arise in such scientific studies.

The Null Hypothesis and Alternative Hypothesis

To every hypothesis there is a second, opposite hypothesis.

- HYPOTHESIS : Smith is leading the election.
  OPPOSITE : Smith is not leading.
- HYPOTHESIS : Drug A is ineffective.
  OPPOSITE : Drug A is effective.
- HYPOTHESIS : Defendant Johnson is innocent.
  OPPOSITE : Defendant Johnson is guilty.

> A hypothesis test is a statistical method for deciding whether you can, with confidence, accept a tested hypothesis.

Of course since you are using statistical methods, you might reject something that turns out to have been correct. In some cases this can be disastrous: You don't want to accidently put an ineffective drug on the market or convict an innocent person. For this reason, one of the two possible hypothesis you are considering gets a special name, the *Null Hypothesis*.

> The Null Hypothesis is the hypothesis that you will stand by unless the statistical evidence is very strong in the other direction.

> The Alternative Hypothesis is the opposite of the Null Hypothesis.

- In a drug test the null hypothesis is that the drug does not help. (You definitely should stick with this assumption unless that evidence is strong that it does help; putting an ineffective drug on the market is disastrous. The alternative is that the drug is effective.
- In a criminal investigation, the null hypothesis is innocence and the alternative hypothesis is guilt. You definitely don't want to convict an innocent person.

The Meaning of Rejection

Here's an important point that often is a source of confusion.

84

> If a hypothesis test points to rejection of the alternative hypothesis, it might not indicate that the null hypothesis is correct or that the alternative hypothesis is false.

In a drug trial a hypothesis test might lead to the rejection of the claim that a drug is effective, even if the evidence is that it *is* effective; the evidence might not be strong enough to take the risk of developing and marketing the drug. In a criminal case, a jury might vote for innocence even though they believe the defendant is guilty; their belief just might not be "beyond a reasonable doubt." A public opinion survey might show that Smith is leading, but the lead might appear so small that Smith should not forgo further campaigning.

p-values

Here we expand briefly on our discussion in Chapter 5.

The set up of a hypothesis test is usually of the following form. An experiment is conducted. If the results vary markedly from what one would expect if the null hypothesis were true, then the null hypothesis is rejected in favor of the alternative hypothesis. Some examples are the following.

☞ A manufacturer claims that the average weight of a part being produced is at least one pound. A fraud officer tests this claim, taking as the null hypothesis that the claim is true. The officer randomly samples 100 parts and finds the average weight is only 14 ounces. Is this sufficient basis to reject the null hypothesis and charge the manufacturer with fraud?

☞ A candidate believes herself to be leading with over 60 percent of voter support in her district. She asks her pollster to confirm this so that she can return to non–campaign duties. The pollster takes as the null hypothesis that the support is really at or below 60 percent. A survey of 500 voters shows support of 63 percent. Is this sufficient to reject the null hypothesis and assure the candidate that she has over 60 percent support?

☞ A pharmaceutical company believes it has discovered a drug that is effective in treating a kind of bacterial infection.

An experimenter for the company sets up to test the claim, making the null hypothesis that the drug is not effective. The drug is given to 20 patients, 40 percent of whom recover. Of 23 patients given a placebo, 35 percent recover. Is this sufficient to reject the null hypothesis and advertise the drug as having a curative effect?

Suppose that in each of these cases the researcher recommends rejecting the null hypothesis. A natural question to ask is how confident the researcher is in making these recommendations. The answer is given by the p-value. To be clear about it, let's state the question precisely in each of the previous three examples.

☞ What is the probability that the average weight is at least one pound and random luck led to the small average of the sample?

☞ What is the probability that my support is less than 60 percent and the randomness of the survey led to the overestimate of 63 percent?

☞ What is the probability that the drug is no better than a placebo and that the small sample and randomness led to its strong showing?

Without knowing more details about each experiment an answer to these questions cannot be calculated, but the following is a conceivable answer to each.

☞ If the null hypothesis is true, the probability of the result being as far off (or more) than occurred in the survey or drug trial is .05.

> Suppose the null hypothesis is rejected on the basis of statistical evidence in favor of the alternative hypothesis. The associated p-value is the probability that the alternative hypothesis would occur when, in fact, the null hypothesis is true.

As we pointed out in Chapter 5, in social science studies a p-value of at most .05 is expected. In medical studies the standard is that the p-value is at most .005. In general:

❖ 7.4. HYPOTHESIS TESTING ❖

> The smaller the p-value, the more convincing the evidence.

⋎ Sometimes you may hear the p-value described as "the probability that the null hypothesis is true." This is not quite correct. The null hypothesis is either true or it isn't. There is no probability associated with this. The probability is associated to the test, which can be repeated, and not to the truth or falsehood of the null hypothesis.

There are cases in which there is a somewhat simpler probabilistic description of hypothesis testing. Here is an example.

☞ Suppose that a pollster sets up the following system. Every time a candidate asks "Do I have at least 50 percent support?" the pollster samples 1,000 voters randomly. If the percentage that respond favorably is at least 53 percent then the pollster responds, "yes, you have at least 50 percent support." A careful computation shows that in cases in which the candidate is not leading, the pollster will falsely claim that the candidate is leading in less than 2.5 percent of the cases.

⋎ Notice that we did not say that the pollster's positive recommendations are wrong 3 percent of the time. For instance, perhaps trailing candidates never happen to use this pollster. Then the pollster's positive recommendations are always correct. At the other extreme, perhaps only trailing candidates use this pollster. In this case all the pollster's positive recommendations are incorrect.

⋎ Notice too that we are not assigning a probability to the possibility that the pollster will falsely accept the null hypothesis. For instance, if the candidate's true support is exactly 53 percent, then the pollster will not find convincing evidence that the candidate is leading in about 50 percent of the cases.

8

Cautions and Fallacies

8.1. Correlation and Causation

We've visited this issue in detail in Chapter 5, but want to emphasize it again.

> Do not confuse correlation with causation.

Simple examples make the correlation versus causation fallacy obvious: The number of people using a public pool correlates highly with the temperature, but we know that encouraging more people to go swimming won't make it hotter. In practice identifying this fallacy is much harder, in that we tend to make the mistake in situations that reinforce popular perceptions.

There have been ample reports connecting drivers' use of cell phones to traffic accidents. Since most of us assume that the added distraction of using a cell phone will lead to inattention to driving, such reports are sure to reinforce our conviction that drivers' use of cell phones does create greater driving risk.

But that argument lacks logic. There may be those hidden third variables, *confounding factors*, lurking in the background. Perhaps it is precisely those drivers who are already at highest risk, those who take caution and attention least seriously, who are the ones who use cell phones. Denying those drivers their cell phones might do nothing to lower accident rates; they will simply find other distractions.

A good statistical study attempts to address these concerns, for instance adjusting for as many confounding factors as possible. But of course, some subjects are not available for statistical study. It is unlikely that someone will undertake a study in which a random sample of drivers is selected and half of them are required to use cell phones while driving and the other half are denied cell phones.

Non-correlation Does Not Imply Non-causation

We should point out that a lack of correlation, or even a negative correlation, does not indicate a lack of causation. For instance, a careful study done at our university showed that students who had taken remedial mathematics courses did no better in physics classes than students who skipped the remedial class. The faulty conclusion was the physics students might as well skip the remedial course. The fact was that *among students with low math SAT scores*, those who took the remedial class did far better in physics than those who did not. It roughly brought them up to the level of those who entered with higher SAT scores. Because of this the low–SAT students became indistinguishable from the rest of the student body and no correlation was detected.

8.2. Beware the Non-random Sample

> If a conclusion is being made about the general population, ask if it is based on a *random* survey or sampling of the general population.

Behind the statistical theory that leads to estimates for such things as the margin of error and correlation coefficients is the underlying assumption that all sampling is random. If a sample is not random, all conclusions become suspect.

This is most obvious with mail–in surveys, such as those done by popular magazines. In this case the readership of the magazine is not a random cross–section of the general population, and those who respond do not represent a random cross–section of the readership.

Telephone surveys, door–to–door interviews, and the like are beset by the same lack of randomness. Unless a survey is undertaken by a trusted organization with a proven track record in accuracy, treat such surveys as representing, at best, the views of the respondents only.

☞ Two kinds of people buy HotBod magazine: those who like the stories and those who like the pictures. A mail–in survey of readers asks a variety of questions concerning the literary tastes of readers (fiction, reportage, etc.) but includes one question regarding the preferred attire on models. Based on this HotBod switches to posing all the models in 18th-century costumes. Big mistake.

There's a way that nonrandomness creeps into statistical studies that is far less obvious than in poorly constructed surveys. Consider the following example.

☞ To encourage sales of its video game SpacePilot, a company has distributed its shareware game JetRaider extensively. A customer surveys finds that 75 percent of SpacePilot buyers were led to it by JetRaider. The conclusion is that by encouraging the distribution of JetRaider, sales of SpacePilot will be boosted as well.

At first this seems logical, though you might wonder if the correlation-versus-causation issue is creeping in here. But let's focus on the lack of randomness. The survey, even if done very well, looked at purchasers of SpacePilot, and hence in no way reflects a random survey of the general game–buying public. In fact, it's possible that a random survey of game–buyers would reveal that distributing JetRaider might actually cut sales. Let's see how this can happen by continuing the example.

☞ Out of 950 game buyers, 900 tried JetRaider, and 90 of those purchased SpacePilot; that's only 10 percent. Of the remaining 50 game players, 30 bought SpacePilot; that's 60 percent. Altogether 120 of the original 950 bought SpacePilot. Of these 120, 90 had tried JetRaider, accounting for the 75 percent result. However, those who tried JetRaider were much less likely to buy SpacePilot than those who didn't try it.

We now see that by surveying only those who did purchase the game, the survey missed the vast majority of the video game buying public.

8.3. A Large Population does not Demand a Large Sample

Suppose that you want to survey the population of a large city concerning an upcoming election. Our results of Chapter 5 indicate that a well designed survey using a random sample of 1,000 voters will produce an estimate with a margin of error of ±3 percentage points.

The same holds true if you are looking into a much larger population, perhaps for a national election.

> Do not discount a survey if it is based on a sample that seems small compared to the over-all size of the group being studied.

For example, a sample of 1,000 is just as effective and ac-curate with a group of million as it is for twenty thousand. The only proviso is that carrying out the random sample with a million people may be more difficult that with the group of ten thousand.

There's no hard and fast rule here; in each case you have to decide whether the survey represented a truly random sam-ple. In the case of professionally done surveys such as those done by Gallup or news groups, you can look to their past successes, or failures, to assess the quality of their surveying methods.

8.4. Comparing Numbers versus Comparing Percentages

> Always ask yourself whether it is better to com-pare raw numbers or percentages.

Imagine the headline: 2000 CENSUS REVEALS MINORITY POPULATION AT ALL TIME HIGH. Here's the story.

☞ New data from the Census Bureau reveals that in 2000 the minority population in Smalltown stood at 500, up from 400 in 1990.

Here's what's missing.

☞ With the 33 percent growth in Smalltown population from 3,000 to 4,000 over the same period of time, this change in minority population represented a drop in minority representation, from 13.3 percent to 12.5 percent.

There's no hard and fast rule for when to use numbers and when to use percentages. But beware: the two can give very different perspectives on the situation. In each situation, ask yourself, what's more newsworthy, the percentage or the total numbers?

8.5. Percentage Change versus Percentage Point Change

Consider the following example:

☞ A drug test shows that 5 percent of individuals who take drug Z see an improvement, while only 4 percent of those who take a placebo see an improvement.

The drug manufacturer might describe this as "Drug Z has been proven to be 25 percent better than a placebo." That sounds like a lot; in this case the percent change is disguising that Drug Z is only 1 percentage point better than a placebo.

As in the case of comparing percentages to raw numbers, there are no hard and fast rules here. We can only advise you to look at the situation carefully and use a description that most clearly describes the situation.

8.6. Regression to the Mean

> Don't identify a movement of the general population toward the mean based on the behavior of the extremes.

Here's an example from baseball.

☞ There were 53 outfielders in the American League who played at least 20 games in both the 2000 and 2001 seasons. In 2000 the mean of their batting averages was .276. In 2001 that mean had fallen slightly, to .262.

If one looks only at the top 15 batters from 2000, their mean batting average fell all the way from .311 down to .269; The lowest 15 batters of 2000 found their mean batting average climbing from .238 all the way up to .260.

Now that's regression toward the mean! The top batters and the bottom batters from 2000 all ended up close to the mean in 2001. The fallacy is to conclude that in 2001 there wasn't much spread between the players. In fact, the spread remained about the same (the standard deviation was in fact almost unchanged). For all the top players who saw their averages fall in 2001 there where players in 2000 who saw their 2001 averages jump way up. (For instance, Juan Gonzalez climbed from a .289 to a .325, Marty Cordova went from .245 to .301, and Adrian Beltran jumped from .247 to .306.)

8.7. Nonexistent Trends

Journalists often follow the tradition that "once is by chance, twice a coincidence, and three times a trend." But beware. Even with events that are occurring completely randomly, now and then strings will appear that in no way predict future of frequent occurrences.

Let's begin with a mathematical example.

☞ A favorite classroom demonstration in a statistics courses has the instructor divide the class into two groups. Each student in one group generates a random sequence of heads and tails by tossing a coin 100 times. Each student in the other group is asked to write down a sequence of 100 heads and tails that looks random, but to skip the actual randomizing using the coin. The teacher is then able to identify by examining the sequences which ones were generated by coin tossing and which as a mental exercise.

The trick? In a random sequence of 100 tosses, there will almost always be a run of at least five heads or tails. Those who make up their sequence will usually not include such a long run — it "looks" so nonrandom.

The message? In a random sequence of events, expect to find patterns and trends appearing. Even if a stock analyst picks stocks by tossing a coin, she will sometimes beat the averages and sometimes do worse than the average. But there will also be what at first appear to be unusually long strings of years in which she beats the average. That is just a characteristic of randomness.

Here is a more practical example.

☞ Suppose that in Trafficville fatal car accidents are relatively rare, occurring on average about once a month. You would expect that in some months there wouldn't be any such accidents, and in some months as many as two or three fatal accidents will occur. Yet, the probability is about 1/3 that over a ten year span there will be some month in which 5 fatal accidents will occur. While that spate is going on, it might feel like a horrible trend has developed, but in fact, such unlucky strings are ultimately quite likely to happen.

8.8. Probability with Conditions

> The probability of A, given B, is different from the probability of B, given A.

For example, the probability that someone will test positive for a disease given that they already have the disease is far different from the probability that someone who tests positive for the disease actually has it. Let's expand on this.

A test of disease X is developed that is 99 percent accurate, both when giving positive and negative results. For instance, this means that if a patient with disease X takes the test, there is a 99 percent probability the test will return a positive. *It does not mean that if someone tests positive there is a 99 percent he has the disease.*

Suppose for instance that disease X is a rare tropical disease that has never affected anyone in Alaska. If 10,000 Alaskans are tested, about 1 percent, that is, 100 of them, will test positive. How many of those 100 who tested positive actually have the disease? Probably none. The 100 positives are just the expected "false positives."

8.9. Combining Overlapping Quantities

Suppose that a survey reveals that 30 percent of students participate in intramural sports and 10 percent are on an intercollegiate team. Can you conclude that at least 40 percent participate in some kind of sports activity? No. Many of those on intercollegiate teams in one sport are on intramural teams in another sport. You cannot just combine overlapping groups in this way.

This sort of reasoning appears frequently. Suppose one studies shows that walking a few miles a day extends the expected life span by two years, and that swimming three times a week also extends expected life spans by two years. Can you conclude that doing both activities will extend your life span by four years? No. Perhaps each activity makes the same contribution to one's health, so that combining them has absolutely no additional benefit.

8.10. Probability versus Odds

In Chapter 2 we described the basic idea of probability. A very closely related notion is that of odds. The distinction between probability and odds can be subtle, and is further complicated by the varied use of the word "odds." In this extended section we will try to clarify some of the language of odds and probability.

Odds

The word "odds" has a formal mathematical meaning and a different meaning when used in the world of gambling. We start with the mathematical meaning.

The **odds** of an event occurring is given by the ratio of the likelihood of its occurrence and the likelihood of its not occurring.

> To compute the odds of an event occurring, divide the probability of it occurring by the probability of it not occurring.

☞ Suppose that 3 out of 10 cars have a particular defect. The probability of there being a defect is 3/10 and the probability of there not being a defect is 7/10. Hence the odds of there being a defect are $\frac{3}{10} / \frac{7}{10} = 3/7$.

This is usually stated as "the odds are 3–to–7 of a randomly selected car being defective."

Converting Odds to Probability

In a situation in which probability applies but you are given the odds, it is easy to convert back to probability.

> If the odds of success are A-to-B, then the probability of success is $\frac{A}{A+B}$.

☞ The odds that a randomly selected shirt of a particular brand has a defect are 1-to-5. Hence, the probability of a shirt being defective is 1/6. In other words, there is 1 defective shirt for every 5 that are not defective, so 1 out of every 6 is defective.

Odds in Gambling

In many situations involving gambling the payoffs are described in terms of odds. The meaning is very different from the formal mathematical meaning.

In such situations as horse racing or sports betting, the odds are used to indicate the payoff for bets. First, here are some examples to illustrate the meaning.

☞ In the Indiana Derby, KnobbyKnees is paying 2-to-1 to win. This means that if you bet $1 on KnobbyKnees and she wins, you will win $2. That is, you will be paid $2 and also your original $1 bet will be returned.

☞ In the Indiana Derby, BumLeg is paying 8-to-5 to win and you bet $2 on BumLeg. If BumLeg wins you should be paid $8 for every $5 you bet. Because you bet only $\frac{2}{5}$ of $5, you will be paid only $\frac{2}{5}$ of 8, or $3.20. When you go to cash in your ticket you will be given $5.20, the $3.20 winnings and your original $2.

> The odds being paid on a particular bet are NOT the odds of winning.

In some games of chance, such as roulette, the odds of winning are roughly the reverse of the odds being paid. In roulette the odds paid (or the "payout") for a bet on a single number are 35-to-1. (If your number comes up on which you bet $1, you get $35 along with your original $1.) The true odds of winning on a single number in roulette are actually 1-to-37; there are 36 numbers on which to bet, 1 through 36, along with the 0 and 00 options. This small difference between the payout and the true odds is the source of profit for the house.

In other settings, such as horse racing, the odds are not set using probability at all but rather depend on the pattern of bettors. In the case of horse racing the method of setting the odds is called the *parimutuel* system. For example, to determine the odds, or payout, for a bet for a horse to win on a given race, the track first totals all bets to win (on all horses combined). Then it takes out some (usually about 20 percent) for its profit. The track then sets the odds so that whichever horse wins, the entire remaining pot of money will be entirely and exactly distributed to the bettors who placed their bets on the winning horse. (For other wagers, such as place or show, the odds are computed similarly.)

Similarly, in betting on professional sports, the odds (and point spreads) are determined by betting patterns and only are tied to the actual prospects of the teams to the extent that bettors assess those prospects.

Cautions

The distinction between odds and probability can lead to misinterpretations.

☞ For conviction of a particular crime, 97 percent of men are sentenced to jail and 95 percent of women are sentenced to jail. Clearly, the results are quite similar.

Consider the odds instead. The odds that a man will go to jail are 97 to 3, or 32.3, whereas the odds that a woman will go to jail are 95 to 5, or 19. *Comparing the two odds alone, it appears that it is far more common that men are sent to jail then that women are sent to jail.* Hence, the odds are significantly higher even though the probability of either a male or female being jailed are similarly very high.

chapter

9

Excel and the Internet

9.1. Web Resources

Sources of Data. There is an ever–growing and rapidly changing body of statistical data readily available on the Internet for the journalist. The U.S. government maintains a website of statistical data called FedStats. The United Nations also maintains large data bases, at the United Nations Statistical Division.

Most university libraries maintain web pages containing lists of sources for statistical data. One of the best is the University of Michigan Document Center.

For sports information, most of the professional sports organizations, such as the NFL, maintain excellent websites.

Sources about Statistics. Here is just one example of a source for information concerning statistics that is available on the Internet:

http://www.dartmouth.edu/~chance/

Every journalist should check out the Chance Newsletter, which is accessible from that site.

9.2. Working with Excel

We will assume here that you are familiar with the basics of working with a spreadsheet such as Microsoft Excel, so we'll discuss only some of the commands and techniques for carrying out descriptive and inferential statistics.

Within Excel there are many shortcuts for performing the

calculations we will describe below. These will be useful to you if you are regularly called on to make statistical calculations. For those of you who are in that situation, we recommend further study of Excel. Similarly, Excel has good graphics capabilities. These too we leave to your own further study.

Our goal here is just to present some of the most fundamental tools that can be useful for the occasional user of statistical calculations and charting.

Basic Cell Notation. We will need to use here the basic notation for referring to a particular cell or group of cells. Here are a few examples.

- C5 refers to the entry in cell C5 (column C, row 5).
- E4:H4 refers to the entries in all the cells in the 4 row from E4 to H4 (E4, F4, G4, H4). Such a horizontal list is referred to as a *row*.
- D5:D9 refers to the entries in all the cells in the D column from D5 to D9 (D5, D6, D7, D8, D9). Such a vertical list is referred to as a *column.*
- C5:E6 refers to the block of cells with corners C5 and E6 (C5, D5, E5, C6, D6, D6, E6).

Basic Measures of a Single List of Numbers. The most common journalistic use of Excel is in computing descriptive statistics about a data set. Suppose that you have a set of numbers, entered in a collection of cells in an Excel spreadsheet.

We assume that your list of numbers is contained in a single column, say in the cells A2 through A15. Usually each row represents a different person or case in the data set, and each column represents a different characteristic. To compute the mean (average), median, or mode, click on an empty cell and enter the appropriate one of the following, not forgetting to include the equals sign (but please ignore the bullet).

- = AVERAGE(A2:A15).
- = MEDIAN(A2:A15).
- = MODE(A2:A15).

If the data are spread among less organized cells, a single command can compute the desired average, incorporating the entries in a column, a row, and two individual cells, and a block of cells. Here is an example:

- = AVERAGE(A3:A11, C4:G4, D5, F3, H3:J7).

Sometimes you may have to compute a standard deviation. In this example, the numbers are contained in the cells in Column C, in rows 1 through 6. The command is:

- = STDEV(C1:C6).

Paired Data. Given two lists of data (with the same number of elements), a single command computes the correlation between the two sets. For instance, suppose that the cells B4 through B50 contain student scores on a midterm exam and cells C4 through C50 contain final exam scores. (Of course, each individual row should contain the midterm and final exam score of the same student.) The correlation coefficient, r, is computed with:

- = CORREL(B4:B50, C4:C50).

⤳ Suppose that an entry is missing from your list; for instance, in a list of weights and heights of individuals, one person's height is missing. Then in computing the correlation, that individual should be ignored in the calculation. It is best that you exclude such individuals beforehand.

Graphics. If you want to add a chart (Pie Chart, Bar Chart, etc.) you will find under the Insert menu the Chart command. A short–cut is to use the Chart Wizard, which may be available in your tools bar. (Excel Help can tell you how to add it to your tool bar if it isn't there already.)

Once you understand the basics of building a chart, the best way to learn how to use Excel to make clear and effective charts is to experiment. Rather than set out with a particular goal in mind, just try out all the available options and see their effects.

Once you create a chart, select it; the Chart menu provides a long list of options for editing your chart.

There are three basic types of chart. Refer to Chapter 3 for information about the design and use of these charts.

Pie Charts. A pie chart can be built from a single list of numbers. Make sure that no cells are selected, or just an empty cell is selected. Then go to Insert menu and select Chart. A dialog box will appear and you should select Pie Chart.

At this point further dialog boxes will appear. The most important asks you for a data range. If you enter a single column of numbers (say C2:C7) you will build the pie chart for that column; it will not have labels. If you pick two adjacent columns (say B2:C7) you will build a pie chart for the data in the second column, with labels coming from the first column.

Table 1 provides an example of a range of cells in an Excel spreadsheet.

Subject	Enrollment
Math	25
English	12
Psych	15
Journalism	5

TABLE 1. Portion of a spreadsheet

If the chart option is chosen and this range of cells is selected, going through the dialogs permits the construction of the pie chart below.

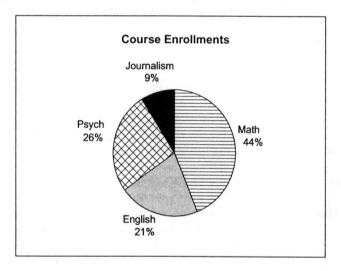

FIGURE 1. A Pie Chart.

NOTE 1. If you build the chart after you select a range, then the chart will automatically be built using that range, which you can edit if you like.

Bar Chart. Bar charts (called "column charts" in Excel) are built in the same way as Pie Charts. The default begins the scale at 0. If you want to use a different scale, select the vertical axis and then go to the Format menu. From that dialog box, select Scale, and proceed from there. By including in your range of cells those that contain labels and using the Chart Options dialog box, a well labeled chart can be built. Here is a sample.

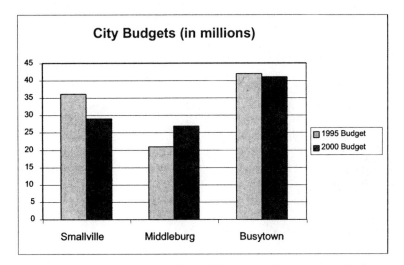

FIGURE 2. A Bar Chart

Line graph. Consider the case in which you are looking at the change of two different amounts over time. To build a line chart, select a region of cells that has three columns: the first should be a label (in this case the year), the second column should give the value of the first quantity and the last column should give the value of the second quantity. The top entry should have the column names in it: this will supply appropriate labels.

↘ When you enter the years in building this chart you must enter them as "words," not numbers, or Excel will assume that this is another series of numbers to be plotted, not the labels for the axis. To do this, instead of typing 1993, type '1993, instead. The single apostrophe tells Excel to treat the 1993 as a label, not as a number.

↘ As you experiment with Excel's charting capabilities you will find a vast array of chart types. Some of these can be quite useful in creating attractive graphic images that will draw your reader's attention and highlight the essential features of the data. But remember too that these same devices can sometimes disguise core information or be so distracting that the reader fails to focus on the essentials.

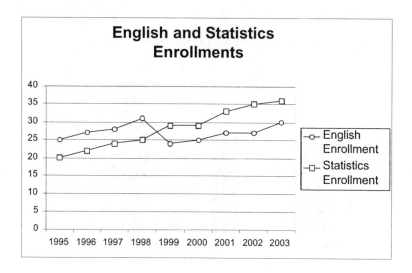

FIGURE 3. A Line Graph.

chapter

10

Writing with Numbers

Most of this book has dealt with basic arithmetic, basic statistics and other mathematical procedures. But none of that will matter if you can't express the math clearly to your readers or listeners. For that reason we'll discuss a few thoughts about writing with numbers.

10.1. Use Numbers — But Sparingly

Many writers we know keep math out of their stories because they think readers' eyes will glaze over at the sight of a number. Actually, numerous readership studies have drawn an interesting conclusion: Given a choice between statistical or numerical facts and the observations of experts and officials, quite often readers and viewers place more credibility with (and prefer to see) the numbers, not the "expert" analysis. Both elements are important to a well reported story, but keep in mind what readers and viewers often prefer.

Compare the following two claims:

☞ Voter turnout on the west side was higher than any other area of the city, and higher than in the previous election.

☞ West-side voter turnout rose from 27 percent two years ago to 39 percent on Tuesday — the highest turnout of any area in the city.

In the first case you've reported a significant fact. In the second you're giving your readers and listeners specific information they can use to draw their own conclusions about the significance of the change. Then, if you added later the turnout percentages of each of the other districts of the city, readers and listeners would have even more useful information.

The trick is to gain a sense of the balance between too few and too many numbers in your copy. The writer's intuitive fear of boring the reader with too many numbers is certainly valid. Consider the following news story:

☞ The council approved a budget that increases police expenditures from $2.4 million to $2.6 million, library spending from $1.1 million to $1.2 million, central administration from $840,000 to $910,000, public works from $1.7 million to $1.9 million, parks and recreation from $725,000 to $780,000 and decreases the fire department allocation from $1.1 million to $980,000.

That's overload. Here's a good, basic rule of thumb.

> Limit a sentence to no more than three numerical values.

If you've got more important quantities to report, break those up into other sentences. More importantly, however, make sure that each number is an important piece of information. Which are the important numbers that truly advance the story? Here's an improvement on the last example.

☞ The council approved a budget providing healthy increases to all the city's major departments but one: the fire department, which will see an 11 percent budget cut.

Better still is the following.

☞ The council approved budget increases ranging from 8 percent to 12 percent for all the city's major departments but one: the fire department, which will see an 11 percent budget cut.

The vague interpretation "healthy" has been replaced with a specific, but not complex, numerical value. The likelihood of glazing over readers' eyes has now dropped sharply, yet the numerical information is nearly as specific, and certainly more helpful, than in the original.

When it is important to present a detailed breakdown of the numerical components of the story, the reporter can create or suggest a graphic to accompany the story.

10.2. **Alternatives to Raw Numbers**

In the example above, the copy improved not only because several numbers were eliminated. It improved because increases in raw numbers (e.g. $1.7 million to $1.9 million) were changed to percentage increases. Writers using numbers often lose readers because the numbers lack context.

Numbers are often useful in stories because they record a recent change in some amount, or because they are being compared with other numbers.

> Percentages, ratios and proportions are often better than raw numbers in establishing a context.

The procedures for figuring percentages, ratios and proportions appear in Chapter 3, but here are a few examples of how these devices can lend clarity to your writing. The following is an OK sentence with some useful information about a baseball team:

☞ The Zephyrs increased their run production this year from 557 to 668 runs.

The reader certainly has enough "raw"information to gauge how great an increase this was for the team, but why make the reader struggle to do some math? The writer can make the comparison obvious by doing a bit of math. Here's an improvement.

☞ The Zephyrs increased their run production this year by 20 percent, scoring 668 runs.

That works better because most people have a sense of what a 20 percent increase is and how significant it is in one year. But there's more a mathematically minded reporter could do to help the story.

The quantity "668 runs" is abstract and not terribly meaningful for baseball fans. Knowing that the Zephyrs' baseball season had 132 games, however, enables a reporter to create a ratio.

☞ The Zephyrs increased their run production this year by 20 percent, from an average of four runs a game to more than five runs a game.

Another example of ratio and proportion is the common task of reporting one part of a whole amount. The following is barely OK.

☞ Of the 3,357 high school seniors in the district, 579 have not yet passed the state's graduation exam.

So how great a problem is that for school officials? Leaving the sentence in that "raw" form presents little context and forces readers and listeners to work out some math in their heads. But the reporter can figure out a proportion to arrive at a better sentence.

☞ One out of every six high school seniors in the district has yet to pass the state's graduation exam.

APPENDIX: This table summarizes the Consumer Price Index for all urban areas for the years 1920 to 2004, computed for January of each year. For instance, the CPI in 1953 was 26.6.

Year	0	1	2	3	4	5	6	7	8	9
1920s	19.3	19	16.9	16.8	17.3	17.3	17.9	17.5	17.3	17.1
1930s	17.1	15.9	14.3	12.9	13.2	13.6	13.8	14.1	14.2	14
1940s	13.9	14.1	15.7	16.9	17.4	17.8	18.2	21.5	23.7	24
1950	23.5	25.4	26.5	26.6	26.9	26.7	26.8	27.6	28.6	29
1960s	29.3	29.8	30	30.4	30.9	31.2	31.8	32.9	34.1	35.6
1970s	37.8	39.8	41.1	42.6	46.6	52.1	55.6	58.5	62.5	68.3
1980s	77.8	87	94.3	97.8	101.9	105.5	109.6	111.2	115.7	121.1
1990s	127.4	134.6	138.1	142.6	146.2	150.3	154.4	159.1	161.6	164.3
2000s	168.8	175.1	177.1	181.7	185.2					

TABLE 1. Consumer Price Indices, January

index